AF668662

RADIO JOURNALISM IN INDIA

RADIO JOURNALISM IN INDIA

VARTIKA NANDA
Teacher-in-Charge
Department of Journalism
Lady Shri Ram College
University of Delhi
Email: vartikalsr@gmail.com

KANISHKA PUBLISHERS, DISTRIBUTORS
NEW DELHI 110002

KANISHKA PUBLISHERS, DISTRIBUTORS
4697/5-21A, Ansari Road, Daryaganj
New Delhi -110 002
Phones: 2327 0497, 2328 8285
Fax: 011-2328 8285
E-mail: kanishka_publishing@yahoo.co.in

Radio Journalism in India
First Published 2017
© Author
ISBN: 978-81-8457-798-3

PRINTED IN INDIA

Published by Madan Sachdeva for Kanishka Publishers, Distributors, 4697/5-21A, Ansari Road, Daryaganj, New Delhi-110 002, Typeset by Sunshine Graphics, Delhi, and Printed at Rajdhani Printers, Delhi.

My Word

My association with the world of radio started way back in 1982, when Radio meant the one and only All India Radio, with private radio stations nowhere on the horizon of possibilities.

Those were the days of utter turbulence for Punjab, going through its worst-ever phase of terrorism. All India Radio and Doordarshan, being the authorized public service broadcasters and the most effective, authentic and popular mode of mass communication, were always under scanner of the establishment. They had a difficult role to play, to be politically correct, and yet to have the credibility of connecting with the masses, and also to convey the message honestly and rapidly. As a greenhorn, even then, I could feel that the public service broadcaster had to be very responsible while communicating to the audience of the size and variety of India.

I remember those days when, in spite of being the main and in fact the only face of the programme that I used to anchor, on many occasions, I had to routinely wait at the main gate of Doordarshan for the security checks. We were also told that the security measures in Punjab were much stricter as compared to other, more peaceful parts of India. To my astonishment, many times I saw the security guards checking the water bottles and bags of children of my age, and sometimes those even younger to me. This went on for many years, giving us the impression that even these huge buildings with umpteen security guards does not fall under a secured zone and that the world of communication, as it was then, too require protection.

Those were the days of killings, kidnappings, threats and curfew, an all-pervading sense of fear and insecurity. So many voices could not find utterance, and the media did not have the professed freedom of expression, as enshrined in the Constitution of India.

I very fondly remember those years of All India Radio in Jalandhar, where a lot of emphasis was placed on quality broadcast. One could very clearly see that the political turmoil and constant threats from terrorists had led to extreme degrees of care and apprehension in broadcast. This was the time when one could clearly notice how All India Radio managed to maintain a remarkable balance between reality and the master's voice, and also between the cold, harsh, objective truth and sensitively pitched, non-sensational, responsible journalism. There were many segments of broadcasts and each one of them got equal attention and recognition. Though news and analysis were important, equal attention was given to drama, classical music and other varied forms of entertainment.When I passed the audition in All India Radio, many stalwarts were regular visitors to the station. All these years, many inspiring memories have accumulated in my mind and helped me relate to, while teaching the students of journalism.

My first visit to All India Radio in Delhi was somewhere around 1989. Two striking images are vivid to my mind. One, the All India Radio being stationed at the historical Parliament Street and two, the stone plaque inside the main office documenting the day when Mahatma Gandhi came to the station for the first and the last time. Each image here has a hidden story to tell.

This compilation is dedicated to every student of journalism who wants to explore the world of journalism and mass communication. It is always a painful experience to witness a large number of students generally wanting to do internships or pick up jobs at places which seem to hold a higher brand value and in that list, AIR generally is not to be found. This book is an attempt to make everyone appreciate and realize, that the present and future of journalism cannot even dream to survive without All India Radio. Invariably on my visits to different stations of AIR, I am pleasantly surprised to see the legacy that has been created by numerous unsung and untiring heroes in the field of broadcasting.

All these years, I have been requesting every broadcaster whom I came across, to work on a book on radio journalism for the benefit of the coming generations and also to document the legacy that we are duty-bound to bequeath to future generations of journalists.

Radio broadcasting has travelled a long way since. The Times of India building in Bombay was the site of the first experimental broadcast in 1921, which was heard by Governor George Lloyd. 100 miles away in Pune. The Radio Club of Calcutta was next, to begin the first systematic broadcast in November 1923.

The person chosen to put Indian broadcasting on a new pedestal was Lionel Fielden, who was appointed Controller in 1935. As early as 1937, Fielden pointed out that treating broadcasting like any other governmental activity would not serve the organization, or the establishment, well. He made a remarkable comment in 1937 by saying, "Broadcasting must be impartial, agile, elastic and adaptable... but a government department can be neither." He also opined once that the government was acting out of duty, rather than pleasure. He could clearly see far beyond his times. By the time Fielden left India in 1940, he had become a friend both of Nehru and

Gandhi, got endorsement of the name "All India Radio", and had overseen the opening of stations in six towns in India, as it was then. There were said to be 100,000 radio households in a population of 400 million people. In 1947, AIR inherited 14 radio stations, a short-wave service and a mechanism for official censorship, as a still very relevant relic of the Raj.

According to Nalin Mehta, a noted media academic and journalist, there are three reasons for the slow growth of radio and TV in India:

1. Restrictive policies inherited from a colonial state
2. Puritanism of the Gandhian national movement, and its aftermath
3. The fear made vivid by the 1947 partition, and of inflaming social conflict

Field enwanted the Radio to grow. In his early years in India, he defied a government order preventing him from meeting Gandhi and attempted to induce the Mahatma to broadcast. However, Gandhi had a very clear opinion. He wrote, "You know and I know that if I do so, I shall increase the number of your listeners overnight by 4 to 5 millions. If I knew you were going to stay in India, I might do it. If you don't, I shall merely increase the strength of my enemies." Mahatma Gandhi's first and only visit to All India Radio studio was, in fact, for addressing the refugees from Pakistan stationed in the refugee camp in Kurukshetra. Nehru's reactions were also similar. Nationalist leaders refused to broadcast on AIR, until Independence had been promised and an interim government had been set up.

At the time of Independence, the infrastructure of media landscape consisted of a handful of popular newspapers, a state-run radio, a commercial film industry and a films division. In the very nascent and formative years itself, India politicians understood the power of Radio. As a famous quote says, 'Politicians want to use radio like a bullet–have a message, fire it and expect the target to be hit." News on Radio was considered as the last word, and had unmatched credibility (and it enjoys this status even now, to the vast millennia in our country's hinterland, especially the impoverished). Thus, it was considered important to make use of Radio as a 'powerful instrument' with the conviction to keep Radio in the 'safe hands of the government.'

In those years of turmoil, Nehru had understood that Radio was more appropriate, and should be better used, for India's stage of development. With Narendra Modi coming to power, one can once again see the power of Radio reaching new heights and connects, specifically so with his regular broadcasts on AIR under the title, 'Mann ki Baat', which no other Prime Minister having thought of it.

I am, in all humility, attempting this book with very inadequate understanding and knowledge of Radio broadcasting. The objective is to compile whatever possible, related to Radio journalism for the benefit of the students of journalism, so that they can peep into the hitherto unexplored world of Radio journalism. All through these years, All India Radio has walked the path with grace, objectivity and dignity and Iam hopeful that this book will open the wide spectrum of that golden era to the audience that is tuned to the Radio, but perhaps is not very accustomed as yet to the world of magic that is All India Radio.

Happy reading!

Dr. Vartika Nanda

Contents

Contents

1

Radio for Education

Dr. O.P. Dewal

Education is emerging from narrow confines of classrooms and campuses to the wider universe. It can now be offered through various communication media and networks. The potential of modern communication technologies has a direct bearing on teaching learning process. If thoughtfully and judiciously used, communication technologies can massively and meaningfully extend educational opportunities and improve the quality of education.

Radio has played a vital role in imparting education at all levels. What is the role of radio in providing education and enrichment in present times will be discussed is this chapter, highlighting the new initiatives taken in this regard.

Historical Perspective

The Spectrum of opportunities for learning in India has gone though a sea change in the past half a century, more so after the advent of twenty-first century. Many technological advances have made the access of the common man more affordable to technology and thus affecting learning patterns deeply and drastically.

Associate Professor, School of Journalism and New Media Studies (SOJNMS), Indira Gandhi National Open University (IGNOU), Maidan Garhi, New Delhi-110068 E-mail: opdewal@gmail.com

It is quite evident today that traditional schooling and formal education system alone cannot solve the problem of mass illiteracy. In majority of the developing countries huge population and limited resources hinder the concept of 'Education for All'. These growing economies need skilled and trained human power, which cannot be provided merely through conventional education system. Some of the significant changes that confront educational planners and managers are increasingly large number of people seeking higher education and training, emergence of new and diverse learner groups, changing learner characteristics and the ways of teaching and learning.

Uses for radio in education fall naturally into three broad categories: improving educational quality and relevance; lowering educational costs and improving access to education, particularly in rural areas.

On World Radio Day 2017, Prime Minister Shri Narendra Modi wrote on Twitter "Radio is a wonderful way to interact, learn and communicate. My own 'Mann Ki Baat' experience has connected me with people across India."

Almost from the time radio was invented there has been a lot of interest in its potential educational role, and by the late 1920s and 1930s a number of educational institutions in Europe, America, and elsewhere were making extensive use of radio. In India when regular broadcasting started in July 1927, like anywhere else, it had three major objectives to fulfill – to inform, to educate and to entertain. All along the twentieth century the first two i.e. information and education remained areas of prime importance.

Organized school broadcasting started in Kolkata in 1937 followed by Delhi, Chennai and other primary channel stations of AIR. After independence educational broadcasting (EB) got the much need impetus. The objectives of EB were to supplement the school curriculum, to support the class teacher and to provide information to students in both urban and rural areas in an absorbing and interesting manner. Funds were allotted to schools to buy radio sets. Later on the educational broadcasting also took higher education in its ambit and started broadcasting programmes for under graduate & post graduate students.

Central Institute of Educational Technology (CIET), a wing of NCERT and various State Institutes of Education have played prominent role in preparing the software for educational broadcasting. Central Institute of English & Foreign Languages (CIEFL), Hyderabad, prepared radio lessons in English language for school children which were broadcast from different stations for duration of 20 minutes and repeated once in a day. Various other agencies were also engaged in planning and production of educational programmes for the primary and the secondary level students which used to broadcast by different stations of AIR.

The curriculum based radio broadcasting got a fillip in our country when the Correspondence education system transformed into Open & Distance Learning. As distance education adopts a multiple media approach for teaching-learning, thereby making radio & television as the important vehicles of knowledge delivery. With the establishment of the first national Open University of India i.e. Indira Gandhi National Open University in 1985, a new era began in the area of educational broadcasting. IGNOU stared its broadcast from three stations of All India Radio in 1991. In less than a decade (in 2001), there was a time when IGNOU Hour programme used to broadcast simultaneously from more than 180 stations of All India Radio at the same time. IGNOU produced a number of audio lesson for its students.

At the International level there were many schemes and projects of Radio Broadcasting which proved to be very successful like The Nicaragua Radio Mathematics Projects, Mexico's Radioprimaria or Teacher Training through Radio in Kenya.

What is Educational Programme

What makes a programme educational? In what ways is it different from the general programmes of information? You may say that prgrammes of information lead to knowledge and one can always learn something from them. Lionel Fieldon, the father of Indian broadcasting, chose mostly teachers and educationists for the senior positions in All India Radio as he had the conviction that people with educational background would invest the broadcasting service with an educational character.

Educational programmes can be broadly classified as, core-curriculum based and enrichment type.

1. *Core-Curriculum Based*:-Educational programmes which are curriculum based focus on the classroom syllabus and deal with various aspects of a subjects.
2. *Enrichment Type*:-Enrichment type programmes are broad based and provide a great deal of supplementary information. They are motivational in nature and try to broaden the horizons and create the appetite for more knowledge. They can also help in promoting the knowledge of a language.

As we all know radio is a sound medium. The message is codified either in terms of sound or pause. We convey everything through them. Even a melodramatic act has to be conveyed through the sound or words only. The sound could be in the form of spoken words, i.e. the dialogues uttered by a character or by sound effects which create an illusion of actual thing or event. Therefore the language used in the programme must be "spoken language" with an informal and natural style. It should be simple and understandable having short and simple sentences. Limited use of statistics is desirable as one cannot remember or digest figures in one go. Theme and style of a programme should be suitable to the broadcast media so as to exploit the potential of the medium. It must be suitable for the audience it is being targeted to. An interesting programme means it will have one or more than one of the following attributes:

- It affects the lives of listeners. It relates to them in some way so that they feel involved. It may concern their livelihood, their environment or just about people, their activity and their emotions.

- There is some conflict: between people, between man and nature, between different ideas, between nations. It may bring out a controversy, a contrast or a clash of some sort. May be a struggle or a problem to be solved or even a challenging question. Conflict normally stimulates interest.
- The programme participants have to be enthusiastic and sound interested. Enthusiasm is needed to arouse enthusiasm.
- The programme is comprehensible to audience. It will also try to create concrete images avoiding abstractions as complexity leads to confusion not interest.

If it is meant for a very large audience and you cannot be so specific then try to pitch your programme at the middle so that it could be enjoyed equally by people at the opposite ends of the spectrum. General audience for any common programme is a very heterogeneous group, especially in a country like India which is so vast and diverse. While looking at the composition of your audience you will also have to analyze their need and supply right kind of product which is in demand.

At the same time you must also remember that sometimes you will have to supply a different kind of product looking at the larger interest of society or nation. In that case you will design your programme in such a way to create its demand. Like all the other mass media radio has also a dual role to play i.e. reflecting the opinion of masses and also building or modifying that opinion.

In radio language, the word 'Format' is used to refer to the form of the programme like the talk format, the story format, the feature format and so on. These formats can be used individually or in combination to make radio programme. The selection of formats depends not on the novelty of the format but on its suitability to express a given idea to a given audience. As is obvious, many of the formats get their names from their usage in literature e.g. story, drama;

but nomenclatures such as feature and documentary have their origin elsewhere.

Radio programmes can broadly be divided into two major categories:

1. The spoken word programmes
2. Music programmes

Mostly the educational programmes fall under the category of spoken word and the major formats used for such programmes are:

1. Talk
2. Dialogue
3. Interview
4. Symposium
5. Panel Discussion
6. Quiz
7. Feature
8. Documentary
9. Drama

Considering the nature and purpose of a programme there could be three types of Educational Broadcasting:

Formal:-Use of Broadcasting media for instructional objective that conforms with the characteristic of formal education like formal curriculum, school hours and grading system etc.

Non Formal:-Used for skilled development of adults without removing them from their workday routine. It involves adult literacy or functional knowledge.

Informal:-Refers to encounter with radio programmes that help individuals to acquire knowledge, however the individual did not set out to acquire it.

Why Radio

Each medium has its own characteristics that make it useful in particular circumstances therefore selection of a particular media for a particular component of courseware is important.

There are also right and wrong ways to use a medium. It should be used in such a manner so that its unique features are appropriately exploited. A poorly designed courseware will fail, even if it was the most appropriate medium. Criteria for Media Selection could be Topic, Objectives, Target Audience, Norms, Funds or Facility.

In audio you have to create pictures through the creative and effective use of words, music and sound for a target audience, which is large and varied. Since it involves your brain to create images all the time, therefore it is called Hot medium or Active medium. The audio communication has to draw upon the basic skills of verbal expression and mould it to suit the listening capability of its audience, i.e., the listeners. An audio programme has to be clear and complete in itself so that the listener should not require any illustration to fully appreciate or understand the message. The language used in the programme must be spoken language with an informal and natural touch.

Some institutions use radio and television broadcasts as adjuncts to printed materials. The strength of such a media mix is that it costs little to the students and can reach out to a large number. The weakness of this arrangement is that the messages are ephemeral, and students do not have any flexibility and control to refer back to the information presented. Furthermore, students receive the message passively, and there is no active interaction between students and the content of learning. Sometimes the broadcasts are at inconvenient times and students find it difficult to view programmes at that hour. Therefore repeat broadcasts are always necessary.

Radio can improve educational quality and relevance, lower educational costs and improve access to education, particularly for disadvantaged groups. It is most effective when supported by trained facilitators, group learning, group discussion, feedback and the use of multiple media approach. There is no single ideal format for educational radio. Innovative programming like those developed by Sesame

Workshop in Africa, offer some very effective approaches to non-formal education over radio

Few Initiatives

- A project entitle the Radio Pilot Project, was started in 1979-80, jointly by the department of Education (Government of Rajasthan), AIR Jaipur and the NCERT, Delhi. The aim of the project was to teach Hindi language to the primary school children. The Radio programmes were planned as part of a package which included print, materials and classroom teacher support.
- In District Primary Education Programme, (DPEP) pilot project entitled, The Radio Project, Vizag, Radio was used to cover 15250 primary schools in the year 2002.
- Radio was used in two educationally backward districts, Gulbarge and Raichur in Karnataka Radio Project of DPEP, during 2000-2001.

Gyan Vani

Gyan Vani opened new vistas in the field of educational broadcasting in the country when the first station at Allahabad went on the air on November 7, 2001. Gyan Vani is the only exclusive educational FM Radio network. In 2013 it was operating through 37 FM stations spread all over the country. Each station has a range of about 70 kilometers and serves the social and educational needs of the people living in that geographical area.

The vision of Gyan Vani is to bring about educational and social development of the community through radio. It seeks greater empowerment of the people, particularly the disadvantaged and physically challenged through their participation. Gyan Vani programmes and interactive sessions are broadly educational in content and character. Programmes, besides covering conventional disciplines and subjects also touch themes such as human rights, consumer education, environmental and ecological issues, value education, career counseling, guidance for competitive exams etc.

Operating as a media cooperative, Gyan Vani is mandated to carve out for itself a distinct identity, different from commercial channels through a different approach and philosophy. Each station is an independently functioning set up with sufficient autonomy and guided by a local steering committee of representatives from different stakeholders. Central linkages are only for policy planning monitoring, budgetary and administrative support.

Stakeholders in Gyan Vani are educational institutions and number of other organizations including NGOs working in the field of education and development. The programme output of each station includes the software generated and contributed by these organizations. IGNOU and other institutions like UGC, AICTE, NCERT, NIOS, NLM, and State Open Universities also offer software. These are supplemented by local productions and acquired programmes from private producers and production companies. Educational organizations located within the listening range of a Gyan Vani station are their active partners.

The Gyan Vani Service got discontinued in 2014 but now it has resumed in 2017 and Delhi and Varanasi stations are again operational.

Interactive Radio Counselling

Effective teaching learning process requires two way communication whereas Broadcast media, by its vary nature, are one way media and offer little scope for two way communication. In past few years with the technological advancement and innovative production techniques and strategies, many initiatives were taken to increase interactivity in Broadcast media. Radio Counselling is one of them.

In May, 1998, IGNOU in co-operation with the All India Radio (AIR) started the pilot project of 'phone-in' counseling from AIR Bhopal. The project objective was to assess the effectiveness of interactive radio counseling. In April 2000, it was extended to 84 Stations of AIR out of which 76 were Local Stations. Later it culminated into full-fledged Interactive Radio-Counseling (IRC) service, provided for an hour from 186 Radio Stations of AIR every Sunday. Toll-free telephone facility was available from 80 cities across the country to enable learners to interact freely with experts and seek clarification on phone.

Now this service is being offered through Gyan Vani in a limited manner.

Here it would not be out of context to consider a few tips for effective utilizations of Interactive Radio Counselling:

a. General

- Always keep your target audience in focus. It means you should know your audiences and the conditions in which the programmes will be received in the schools or homes. Never forget whom you are talking to.
- The first responsibility of the men women behind the mike is to communicate in an intelligible way. Hence, the radio performer needs to develop and refine his/her speaking skills – articulation, enunciation, pronunciation, variety, intonation and naturalness.
- Speak as if your are talking to a friend-an equal and intelligent person, never talk at or talk down to your listeners. Radio is for telling and for talking-person to person. So, always imagine a friend's face on the microphone and then talk to him or her. Further you may have thousands of listeners, but always talk as if you are addressing one person.
- Try to have a smile and warmth in your tone as you speak into the microphone. You know that you have only the medium of sound to convey your message so act a little and try to put everything in your voice-interest, excitement, humor, surprise, and above all a personal touch. Remember a smile can be heard.

b. For the Anchor Person/Moderator

- Introduce the theme and resource persons for the session in progress.
- Announce Telephone & Fax numbers. Instruct the viewers from time to time
- Invite questions from the viewers and to decide the order of responses to these questions.
- Keep track of the time and to wind up the session by thanking the experts and the participants.
- Announce the theme, and the time of the next session.
- During the broadcast if there is no interaction with the students, anchor should be ready with some question to make the session interactive/live.
- Anchor should try to bunch the questions and look for the suitable point for interaction; also s/he should follow up if the answer in not complete.
- Anchor should summarize the content in the end, preferably point wise.

c. For Participant/Resource Persons

- Use a participatory style of presentation and use a friendly tone. Imagine that you are in a group discussion talking to a small group of persons. Avoid lecturing as is to a large audience. Use conversational language.

Audio Books

An audio book is audio recording of the printed paper book, which could be fiction or non-fiction, and it is read by a professional narrator or a voice over artist. Sometimes, the narrator can be the author. The audio book can have more than one narrator which depends upon the cast, and can be embellished with sound effects to reflect the mood or the scene of the story.

Audio books audience is wide and large. Audio books are not only for people with physical disabilities but also for everyone. Particularly for people who do multi-tasking. For those who find it easier to learn by listening in their comfort zone. Audio books are not only for people with diminished eye-sight but also for those who want to do more than one thing at the same time. Audio books are a handy way for people to know about a subject while jogging, driving, cooking, or by easing oneself and learn about something.

There is growing market for audio books in the industry. They are available in all genres: fiction, non-fiction, children's books, self-help books, etc. Books published in the print format are also available in the form of audio books. For example: Ulysses written by James Joyce, one of the longest stories in novel format – running into 933 pages and published in 1922 – is now available in an audio book format. It is common to find audio books in bookshops, supermarkets and also on online platform. The trend is also catching up in India. Kiss & Tell, a novel written by Nistula Hebbar and published in 2012, is not only available in the book format but also as an audio book.

Internet Radio

When radio signals are made available through streaming, on the internet, to reach the listener, it is called Internet radio or Web radio. Internet Radio has made it possible to engage listeners (in this case learners) globally and that too 24x7, at the time and place of their choice. National Institute of Open Schooling (NIOS) used the services of Internet Radio & Community Radio for reaching their students.

Community Radio and Campus Radio

Community radio can be defined as a radio service that offers a third model of radio broadcasting in addition to commercial and public broadcasting. Community radio stations serve geographical communities and communities of interest. Community broadcasting is broadcasting which is for, by and about the community, whose ownership and management is representative of the community, which pursues a social development agenda, and which is non-profit. It is another mechanism through which programmes related to education and development broadcast for a very focused and targeted group of listeners.

The Community Radio Policy was enacted in 2002, and a set of Revised Policy Guidelines issued in 2006. The persistence in demand by social change and media activists brought in a more progressive and inclusive policy for CR in 2006. The new guidelines allowed non-governmental organizations to establish CR stations. These radio stations broadcast content that is popular and relevant to a local, specific audience but is often overlooked by commercial broadcasters. Community radio stations are operated, owned and influenced by the communities they serve.

The Community Radio which is operated by an educational institution is called a Campus Radio. This type of Radio service is highly useful for the purpose of educational broadcasting as one of the communities in the vicinity of any educational institution are students. Presently more than 100 Campus Radios are operational in our country and broadcasting meaningful educational programmes for the students and teachers.

From all the experiments and experiences, the importance of Radio in education and development seems to be definite and proven. What is needed is innovation in the software production and ground level preparedness.

REFERENCES

Daniel, John S. (1996) Mega Universities and Knowledge Media: Technological Strategies for Higher Education, London: Kogan Page

Kumar K.L. (1996) Educational Technology, New Delhi, New Age International Private Ltd., p. 306.

Roll, Reidar (1998) International Trends in Open and Distance Learning, Open Ideas, Warangal,: IDEA, vol.6,No.1.

Sharma G.D. (2005) Knowledge Packaging for Face to Face and Self Paced Learning, Reading Material on Development of E-Content on Higher Education, CEC, New Delhi.

Singh & Sudarshan (2006) Broadcasting Education, New Delhi, Discovery Publishing House

Sreedher, R (1999) Interactive Radio Counseling: the AIR-IGNOU experience. Paper presented at the AAOU conference at China in 1999.

2

Private FM Radio: Policy Perspective and Contemporary Issues

Dr. Ambrish Saxena

Private FM (Frequency Modulation) radio broadcasting focuses on narrowcasting as different from MW (Medium Wave) and SW (Short Wave) broadcasting of AIR (All India Radio). Private FM broadcasting has a defined area and a targeted listeners' group. The target of the private FM radio [as per policy announced in 2000] is to expand radio all across urban areas [but confining a radio channel to the allotted city] of the country, and to infuse new blood in programme content and presentation in view of changing aspirations, interests and patterns of media use in 21st century.

In Private FM radio, the audience is to be identified not only on demographic basis but also on psychographic basis. This means that these radio stations target a particular segment i.e. youth in a geographical location i.e. city. Here, an attempt

Dr. Ambrish Saxena is Professor and Academic Head, Zee Institute of Media Arts (ZIMA) and Zee Institute of Creative Arts (ZICA), a venture of Zee Learn Limited (ZLL) in collaboration with Zee Media Corporation Limited (ZMCL). Earlier, he has been Director, Vivekananda School of Journalism and Mass Communication (VSJMC) and Dean, Research and Publication, at Vivekananda Institute of Professional Studies (VIPS), and Professor and Consultant, Centre for Media Studies, GGS IP University, Delhi.

has been made to understand the Private FM broadcasting in India in the backdrop of policies and implementation on those policies. This study goes deep into the policymaking, the shortfalls in the policy, the success rate of the policy, the implications and the current scenario as also the future prospects.

Private FM Radio: Studying Thrust of Policy

Beginning of FM in India

The first city centric channel of All India Radio based on FM technology was commissioned in Jalandhar in 1992 and in Delhi in 1993. These FM channels came to be known as 'AIR FM Stereo' because of stereophonic sound quality of FM. The second city centric channel of AIR based on FM technology was launched in Delhi in 2001, following which the first channel became FM 1 [Now, AIR FM Rainbow] and the new channel became FM 2 [Now, AIR FM Gold]. Thus, the identity of AIR FM channels was linked to the technology which was being used for the purpose of transmission.

In view of proven quality of FM technology, AIR has shifted many of its Vividh Bharati channels and primary channels from MW to FM, and this process continues. FM mode of transmission is, in fact, being used for all kind of channels, from AIR channels to private channels and from local radio stations to educational channels.

The objective of studying the policy perspective of private FM radio broadcasting is to find out thrust of the policy, to understand the initiative taken and the process adopted for the formulation of the policy, and to analyse implementation on and success of the policy.

Policy Documents Related to Private FM

For understanding private FM radio in a better light the reports of the Tenth Five Year Plan and Eleventh Five Year Plan on the expansion of radio broadcasting need to be referred.

Besides, the following documents need to be referred so as to be update on the policy of private FM radio.

- First Private FM Radio Policy 2000
- Radio Broadcast Policy Committee Report 2003
- Policy on Private FM Phase II 2005
- TRAI Recommendations on Private FM Phase III 2008
- Policy on Private FM Phase III 2011
- Policy revision on Private FM Phase III 2013
- Policy additions on Private FM Phase III 2015

The secondary data used in this study has been collected through the following sources.

- TRAI consultation papers and recommendations [As available on their website]
- Recommendations made by GOMs and EGOMs [As available on website of Ministry of Information & Broadcasting]
- Policy approvals by the cabinet [As available on website of Ministry of I & B]
- Newspaper reports [As available on their web pages]
- Other websites and news portals

Beginning of City Centric FM Broadcasting

City centric FM radio broadcasting started in 1992, and it was part of partial radio privatization policy of the government. As part of this policy, AIR opened up its FM channels in cities and outsourced their programmes to private programme production companies in different time slots. The fill-fledged privatization happened in 2000 when private operators were given licenses for running FM radio channels in cities.

Entry of Private Players on AIR FM Channels

The first ever city centric FM channel was commissioned at Jalandhar on October 2, 1992 and within a year's time FM channels came up in Delhi, Mumbai, Chennai, Panaji and Kolkata. The government decided to introduce partial privatization in FM broadcasting and accordingly AIR started leasing out time slots to private operators on its FM channels. Nine time slots were leased out on AIR FM channels (later named as Rainbow) of Delhi and Mumbai on August 15, 1993. Time slots were given to private operators in Chennai on September 1, 1993, Panji on January 24, 1994, and Kolkata on July 25, 1994.

With innovate programming and aggressive marketing, efforts of private parties brought FM to the centre stage. However, they ceased to operate the slots with effect from June 26, 1998 as the government was contemplating full-fledged privatisation of FM broadcasting, enabling private parties to set up and operate FM stations. At least this was on record though the confrontation between private programme producing companies and AIR programming heads was not a secret.

There was evidently a clash in the value system of AIR and that of private players. AIR was too possessive for its Broadcast Code and persistently asked the private production companies to adhere to the code while producing the programmes. Despite the agreement in that respect the private players were not too willing to follow the code. This created a mismatch between the programmes produced by AIR and those produced by private companies during the course of broadcasting. Repeated controversies led to a legal tussle and finally the ties were broken between AIR and private players.

Beginning Made in Ninth Five Year Plan

The formal beginning of privatisation policy was made in Ninth Five Year Plan (1997-2002) objective. In this plan, the policy objective for radio was improving the variety of content and technical quality of broadcasting. On the technological front the focus shifted from Medium Wave to Frequency Modulation.

During the Plan Period the thrust areas for radio were on:

- Improvement of programme content

- Providing wider choice of programme
- Improving broadcast quality
- Enhancing technical features
- Renewal of old and obsolete equipments
- Addition of new facilities at radio stations

First Phase of Private FM Broadcasting

In pursuance of the Ninth Five Year Plan (1997-2002) objective, the government allowed fully owned Indian companies to set up private FM radio stations on license fee basis. The decision to open up the frequencies to private participation was taken by the government with the following objectives:

- To open up FM broadcasting for entertainment, education and information dissemination by commercial broadcasters
- To make available quality programmes with a localized flavour in terms of content and relevance
- To encourage new talent and generate employment opportunities directly and indirectly
- To supplement the services of All India Radio (AIR) and promote rapid expansion of the broadcast network in the country for the benefit of the Indian populace

In May 2000, 108 frequencies in the FM spectrum (VHF 87-108 MHZ) were auctioned across 40 cities (later categorized as A+ cities) in the country through an Open Auction Bidding process. Multiple round auction mechanism was followed to award these licenses. The award of licenses was made on the basis of cities. These cities were divided into five categories on the basis of the amount of reserve license fees.

The government received 101 bids for an aggregate of Rs 425 crores as against the estimated amount of Rs 79.65 crores from bids for 37 frequencies as bidders for other frequencies defaulted. A total of 37 licenses were issues on city basis for a period of 10 years, with the provision of escalation in license fee @15% per annum on the base of the first year fees.

Evidently, progress on operational FM radio was very slow. Services could start only in 14 cities and 24 stations (of which 2 were granted deemed operational status). Thus, only 22 licenses could actually become operational though one channel later closed down. Two licensees continued to pay license fees but they failed to float their channels.

The deadline for operationalising the licenses was one year from signing the License Agreement i.e. December 29, 2001. However, ever after furnishing the bank guarantee and signing the License Agreement, 13 successful bidders could not operationalise their licenses within the required time frame and ultimately surrendered their licenses. The first private FM radio channel came up in July 2001.

Failure of First Phase of Private FM

The companies which were given license in the first phase started facing a rough weather since beginning. The private operators met the representatives of Information and Broadcasting Ministry in August 2001 to resolve the contentious issues but the government was of little help. This led to delay in the launch of most of the private FM channels.

In August 2002, the tussle between Information and Broadcasting Ministry and radio operators came in open, the point of controversy being heavy license fee and other unjust conditions imposed on operators. In the wake of this, two companies Millennium Radio- Chennai and Midday Radio-New Delhi walked out of the contract. Other companies also threatened to pull out, while some got involved in litigation.

The result of the first phase of private FM broadcasting was disappointing as only 25 percent of the licenses could become operational. Most of the private operators were finding the projects commercially unviable primarily due to heavy license fee. The private players continued to suffer losses and mounted pressure on the government to amend the policy.

Meanwhile, a working group on Information and Broadcasting sector was set up under Tenth Five Year Plan (2002-2007). This group felt that treating private FM broadcasting services as source of revenue was counterproductive as that could hinder the growth causing delay in the roll out of private FM services. The group recommended that suitable corrective policy measures should be taken, so that future growth of these services could be accelerated and substantial private investment could be attracted to supplement the efforts and investment of All India Radio.

Efforts for Amending Private FM Radio Policy

Despite not very good experience of the first phase of FM broadcasting, the Tenth Five Year Plan envisaged further expansion of private FM radio broadcasting. In view of the opinion expressed by the Planning Commission, and representations by private FM radio operators, the government initiated process for amendment in the private FM radio policy.

Tenth Five Year Plan Emphasis on Expansion of FM

In the Tenth Five year Plan (2002-2007) the broadcasting scenario was reviewed and it was found that MW transmission had reached 99 percent of the population. However, FM broadcasting was found to be the preferred mode of radio transmission all over the world due to its high quality stereophonic sound. Therefore, the emphasis in the Tenth Plan was on substantially enhancing FM coverage from 30 to 60 percent of the population by the end of the plan period.

The following were the major thrust areas of the Tenth Five Year Plan:

(*a*) No further expansion of MW transmission except in sparsely populated, hilly terrain and strategic border areas where it will still be more cost effective

(*b*) Expanding the reach of FM radio to cover 60 percent of the population by the end of the Tenth Plan. Private operators are to be encouraged to provide FM radio services in metros and small cities.

(*c*) Encouraging private participation in providing quality services and replacing the existing system of bidding for licenses with a revenue sharing mechanism

(*d*) Creation of high quality content with long shelf life to enable AIR to fulfill its role of public service broadcaster

(*e*) Strengthening and expanding the reach of radio in the North Eastern states (including Sikkim) and island territories

(*f*) Use of FM radio to spread literacy, because of better transmission and reception

The Tenth Plan stipulated that private operators were to be encouraged to provide FM Radio services in metros and small cities. For the FM license, it also envisaged replacement of the existing system of bidding for license with a revenue sharing mechanism.

Radio Broadcast Policy Committee

The government set up a committee named as Radio Broadcast Policy Committee headed by Dr.AmitMitra, then secretary general of FICCI, on July 24, 2003, to study the private FM broadcasting scenario and give recommendations for the second phase of licensing. The committee, in its report submitted in November 2003, recommended to introduce revenue sharing system between the government and the private players, and also to open up the broadcasting sector to FDI up to 26 percent at par with other media sectors.

Mitra Committee recommended that the license fee structure should be revised and migration of the license terms from fixed license fee basis to one-time entry fee with an annual revenue sharing arrangement should be allowed. The entry fee should be determined by a competitive bid process that will reflect the true market value of the frequency. In addition, there should be an annual revenue share, which was recommended as 4 percent of the gross revenue.

Mitra Committee also made two other important recommendations, *one-* to set up a Universal Service Obligation Fund to support non-commercial channels, and *two-* to use the scarce resource (frequency) rationally, efficiently and optimally.

Recommendations by TRAI on Policy Change

The government could not immediately take a decision on the recommendations of Mitra Committee. Subsequently, Information and Broadcasting Ministry, on February 12, 2004, sent the report of the Mitra Committee to Telecom Regulatory Authority of India (TRAI) for its opinion and recommendations.

It may be noted that the government was required to set up an independent authority to regulate airwaves in the light of the Supreme Court judgment on airwaves in 1995. Further, Paswan Committee also advised the government to set up a regulatory body in 1996. Since the government failed to put a broadcast regulator in place, it decided to give the regulator's job to Telecom Regulatory Authority of India (TRAI) for the time being through a notification on January 18, 2004.

Based on the input received from Information and Broadcasting Ministry, Report of the Radio Broadcast Policy Committee and representations from private FM operators, TRAI prepared a consultation paper on April 14, 2004 and invited comments from all stakeholders. After looking into the viewpoints of stakeholders and the report of the Mitra Committee, TRAI submitted its recommendations on licensing and other issues for the second phase of private FM radio broadcasting in August 2004.

The summary of TRAI recommendations is mentioned below.

- TRAI recommended one-time entry fee and a revenue share (4 percent of the gross revenue of the company) arrangement replacing the earlier licensing procedure.

- TRAI said that the existing ban on multiple licenses in one centre should be given up but added that one entity should not be allowed to hold more than three or one-third of the licenses in one city.
- TRAI refrained making clear recommendations about FDI, cross media ownership and news broadcast, and asked the government to review these issues.
- TRAI permitted no networking within the same city, no networking across licenses, but permitted the same between stations located in different cities belonging to the same broadcasting company.
- TRAI asked the government to make more frequencies available for big as well as small cities, so that more FM station can be opened up.
- TRAI did not make any clear recommendation regarding non-commercial channels. It, however, said that the government may think of creating a separate fund for the purpose of developing non-commercial channels.
- TRAI did not endorse the suggestion of Mitra Committee for setting up niche channels, and said that this can be taken up after the industry stabilizes.
- TRAI said that co-location of all FM transmitters should be mandated in metros; and in case it is not feasible to co-locate all transmitters on a single tower due to various technical reasons, government may allow one or more towers to co-locate the transmitters.
- TRAI permitted Phase I operators to migrate to Phase II conditions, provided that they pay all dues, withdraw all pending litigation and also not be in default of any license condition.

Private FM Radio Phase II Policy

The government accepted most of the TRAI recommendations and came out with a policy announcement on expansion of

FM radio broadcasting services through private agencies (Phase II) on July 13, 2005. The policy provided for granting license to enterprising broadcasters on the basis of One-Time Entry Fee (OTEF) quoted by the bidders (Closed Tender System). The policy also included provisions related to FDI, news broadcast, networking, and migration from Phase I to Phase II.

The policy included the following major provisions.

- All the cities having population equal to or more than 3 lakh were to be considered for the expansion of FM radio broadcasting. These included the metro cities (also covered in Phase I).
- The cities were categorized on the basis of population; metro cities were categorized as A+, cities having population 20 lakh and above as A, cities having population 10 lakh and above as B, cities having population 3 lakh and above as C, and cities having population 1 lakh and above as D.
- The government decided not to include D category cities in Phase II.
- The government changed the licensing procedure and the license fee calculation as compared to Phase I. In the new policy guidelines (mostly based on the recommendations of TRAI), two-stage selection process was adopted. Firstly, eligibility of bidders was determined, and subsequently financial bids were called from eligible bidders.
- Reserve One-Time Entry Fee (OTEF) was fixed at 25 percent of the highest bidding price in the city. Any bid below the reserve limit was to be summarily rejected.
- As per the revenue sharing formula, the permission holder was liable to pay an annual fee @ 4 percent of the gross revenue of the company for each year or 10

percent of the OTEF, whichever was higher. Gross revenue for this purpose would be the gross revenue without deduction of taxes.

- The license was valid for a period of ten years from the date of operationalisation of the channel, with no provision for extension. The government at an appropriate time would determine procedure for issue of fresh permissions and no concessional treatment will be given to the permission holders in the allotment of channels.
- The policy document prescribed no change in the FDI limit of 20 percent, and framed no rules with regard to cross media ownership.
- The policy disapproved the recommendations of TRAI for multiple licenses (to one entity) at one centre. The government adopted the policy of one entity one channel in one city provided the total number of channels allocated to the entity was within the overall ceiling of 15% of all allocated channels in the country.
- No permission holder was allowed to outsource, through any long-term production or procurement arrangement, more than 50% of its total content, of which not more than 25% of its total content was to be outsourced to a single content-provider.
- No permission holder was allowed to hire or lease more than 50% of broadcast equipment on long-term basis.
- Ban on the broadcast of news and current affairs programme continued. The policy document endorsed the Phase I policy of making adherence to AIR Broadcast Code and Commercial Code compulsory to private broadcasters.
- TRAI recommendation of permitting networking across cities (between channels of the same entity) was not accepted by the government. The policy guidelines

permitted an entity to network its channels in C and D category cities within a region only, but did not permit networking by two entities of their channel in any category of cities.

- Co-location of transmission facilities was made compulsory for all the FM operators. In case of inadequacy of AIR/DD towers, new towers had to be constructed by the Ministry of Information and Broadcasting through Broadcast Engineering Consultants India Limited (BECIL) for the purpose of co-location.
- The policy guidelines permitted migration of Phase licenses to Phase II regime subject to fulfillment of certain conditions.

Fresh Efforts for Revamping Private FM Radio

The government initiated the bidding process for Phase II of private FM radio on June 8, 2007. By the end of 2007, 136 channels (including Phase I channels) became operational.

The cities covered in Phase II were having population of more than three lakh, and so a need was felt to cover the cities with lesser population in the next phase.

Recommendations of Sub Group on I& B

The Sub-Group on Information and Broadcasting under Eleventh Five Year Plan (2007-2012) noted that the FM coverage remained at the level of 40 percent by population as against the Tenth Plan target of 60 percent. The Sub-Group emphasized on border area coverage through FM and laid the responsibility of doing this on PrasarBharti. It said that in urban areas private sector can take a lead role.

The Sub-Group recommended that the AIR should go in for digital broadcasting in a big way commencing with the Eleventh Plan using the Digital Radio Modulation (DRM) technology, for Short Wave and Medium Wave as well as FM transmitters compatible with DRM+ technology. The proposal was to increase the coverage from 40 percent to 75 percent by population using DRM+ compatible transmitters for FM. This provided an option of leasing out DRM+ compatible transmitters to private operators.

TRAI Consultations for Phase III

In view of recommendations by the Sub-Group on Information and Broadcasting, the government decided to initiate steps for further revision in private FM radio broadcasting policy. On November 13, 2007, the government made a formal request to TRAI to suggest measures for the third phase of private FM broadcasting. On January 8, 2008, TRAI released a consultation papers and conducted discussions with all stakeholders and experts including FICCI and BECIL for about 10 days. The consultations proved significant in view of finding consensus on issues where opinions were sharply divided.

Through the consultation process TRAI mainly tried to resolve regulatory issues particularly the issues which remained unanswered or untouched in Phase II policy. It may be noted that TRAI, while making recommendations for Phase II, took a deliberate decision of leaving certain issues for consideration under Phase III so that implementation on Phase II could not delay. One major task before TRAI in the third phase was to recommend measures for expansion of FM radio broadcasting to major parts of the country.

Recommendations by TRAI for Phase III

On the basis of comments of stakeholders, internal analysis and available best international practices, TRAI finalised the recommendations on February 22, 2008. Vital issues covered by TRAI in its recommendations included additional FM channels in a district, FDI limits, networking of programmes, and news and current affairs programmes on FM radio. A summary of recommendations follow.

- The geographical basis for bidding should be changed from city to district. In the new system, OTEF should be re-fixed based on the maximum bidding price through the auction for the district. Annual fee is to be determined considering revised reserve OTEF.

- After following the basis of district the availability of frequency will increase. This can help in providing additional channels in A+, A, B and C category cities, as envisaged in Phase II. In D category cities (now changed to district basis) the number of channels may be reduced to three to five.
- Since city basis was not acceptable to the government, TRAI later accepted the viewpoint of the government and agreed to continue the city level licensing in the larger interest of expediting the process.
- At least three channels in any district/ city should be given to three different entities. After this any existing operator may bid for other channels with the condition that maximum number of channels to a permission holder in the district/ city will not be more than 50 percent of total channels in the district/ city.
- FDI limit should be increased from 20 to 26 percent in the case of news channels and to 49 percent in the case of non-news channels.
- FM channels should be allowed to broadcast news but with the condition that they have to take contents from authorized sources.

On the recommendations of TRAI, Ministry of Information and Broadcasting sought some clarifications on November 18, 2008. TRAI responded back with its comments on November 28, 2008.

Phase III Policy on Expansion of Private FM Radio: 2011

In the light of recommendations and clarifications made by TRAI, the government could have launched Phase III policy on expansion of private FM radio in 2009 only but it took too long. A Group of Ministers (GOM) was formed with Finance Minister Pranab Mukherjee in the chair to finalise the policy. The GOM in its meeting on January 22, 2011 approved the policy.

The GOM sent the policy draft to the cabinet which approved the 'Policy Guidelines on Expansion of FM Radio Broadcasting Services through Private Agencies (Phase III)' in its meeting held on July 8, 2011. The meeting decided in favour of online bidding of licenses instead of conventional open bidding process. The government also announced that it may issue approximately 700 licenses in Phase III.

As per the announcement made by the government in July 2011, FM Phase III Policy would cover FM radio services to about 294 new cities, with a total of 839 FM radio Channels. It may be noted that by the end of 2012, 185 radio stations were in operation in 92 cities.

The thrust of Phase III policy is inclusion of D category cities i.e. the cities having below three lakhs but above 1 lakh population. It may be noted that only A+ cities were covered in Phase I whereas A, B and C category cities were added to the list in Phase II. But D category cities remained uncovered in Phase II.

Highlights of Phase III Policy: 2011

The highlights of the Phase III policy follow.

- The long pending demand of the broadcast of news by private FM radio channels has been accepted by the government but with a rider i.e. Channels are permitted carriage of news bulletins of All India Radio. However, the channels are not allowed to produce and broadcast their own news bulletin.
- The line between news and non-news was blurred in Phase I and Phase II policies, but Phase III policy has clarified this issue. Now, the broadcast pertaining to certain categories like information related to sporting events, traffic and weather, coverage of cultural events, festivals, coverage of topics concerning examinations, results, admissions, career counselling, availability of employment opportunities, public

announcements pertaining to civic amenities like electricity, water supply, natural calamities, health alerts etc. as provided by the local administration would be treated as non-news and current affairs broadcast, and would therefore be permissible.

- The limit on the ownership of channels, at the national level, allocated to an entity is retained at 15 percent in the third phase, similar to the cap prescribed in Phase II. However, channels allotted in Jammu & Kashmir, North Eastern States and island territories are allowed over and above the 15% national limit to incentivize the bidding for channels in such areas.
- The city wise limit of owning the channels has also been modified. Private operators are allowed to own more than one channel but not more than 40 percent of the total channels in a city subject to a minimum of three different operators in the city.
- In Phase III, one significant departure from the earlier stand taken by the government is on the FDI limit. The FDI+FII limit in a private FM radio broadcasting company has been increased from 20 percent to 26 percent.
- Phase III has rationalized rules with regard to networking of channels. The new policy permits the networking of channels within a private FM broadcaster's own network across the country instead of only in 'C' and 'D' category cities of a region allowed earlier.
- As proposed in Phase III, private FM broadcasters would have the choice to select any agency other than BECIL for construction of transmission tower within a period of 3 months of issuance of LOI failing which BECIL would automatically become the system integrator and set up co-location facilities.
- The government has decided to take initiative of providing special incentives for North East (NE)

Region and Jammu & Kashmir (J&K) and Island territories.

- Private FM radio operators in North East (NE) Region and Jammu & Kashmir (J&K) and Island territories would be required to pay half the rate of annual license fee for an initial period of three years from the date from which the annual license fee becomes payable and the permission period of fifteen (15) years begins.
- The revised fee structure would be made applicable for a period of three years, from the date of issuance of guidelines, to the existing operators in these states to enable them to effectively compete with the new operators.
- Apart from the fee relaxation, it is further proposed that Prasar Bharati infrastructure would be made available at half the lease rentals for similar category cities in such areas.

Review of Phase III Policy: 2011

The Phase III policy on private FM radio broadcasting as announced in July 2011 was a step in the right direction, though delayed by many years. The new policy brought cheers to Phase II operators as well, since the benefits of policy modifications in Phase III were also to be made available to them. The merits of this policy could be summed up below.

- The existing Phase II operators will be allowed to migrate from Phase II to Phase III. The migration fee will be decided after consultation with telecom regulator TRAI for auction of 3G and broadband wireless access spectrum.
- In order to prevent monopoly, no group will be allowed to have more than 15% of all the channels, except in the North-East, Jammu and Kashmir and some Union Territories.
- The incentives provided in Phase III policy with regard to J&K, North Eastern states and Island

territories would make the operations viable in these areas as more channels might come forward to have their set up. The steps taken in the new policy would bring down operational costs and improve viability in general.

- To improve the viability further as against a maximum of 4 channels in D category cities (prescribed in FM Phase II), the new policy has proposed only 3 FM channels in D category cities. This would reduce fight for limited advertising revenue in a city.
- In Phase III, the lock in period of shareholding of promoters/majority shareholders will be reduced from the present 5 years to 3 years. This would give the operators greater freedom to change the shareholding pattern.
- Phase III policy would allow operators to distinguish themselves from others enabling them to cater to niche audiences. This would happen because of content diversification in view of news content, and also because of the provision of multiple-ownership of channels in a city, with the exception of D category cities. This would also increase the overall listenership base and the listening time.
- The additional channels that may become available due to a reduction in the inter-channel spacing to 400 KHz from the existing 800 KHz could be considered subsequently, after feasibility studies are undertaken in this regard.

Developments in Phase III Policy: 2013

The policy announced in July 2011, despite all its merits, could not be implemented. It was further handed over toempowered group of ministers' (EGOM). The cabinet approved the recommendations of EGOM on May 1, 2013.

Subsequently, the government announced that e-auction will be held for 839 FM radio channels in 294 cities through private agencies. It was decided that new FM radio frequencies will be opened for cities with a population of above one lakh which means primarily D categories. Besides, vacancies in other category of cities were also to be filled up.

The most important aspect of this new Phase III policy is e-auction for the channels which is be conducted in batches. The number of batches is to be decided by Information and Broadcasting Ministry, depending upon the response from the bidders after auction of first batch. The Ministry of I &B is to appoint an independent expert agency, through a transparent selection process, following established procedure, to conduct e-auction.

The Ministry decided to separately issue a detailed Information Memorandum, in due course, enabling the prospective bidders to participate, and also indicating the cities, reserve prices city-wise, number of channels to be taken up in each batch and other procedures for e-auction. It was also decided to issue in due course of time a Notice Inviting Applications (NIA) for participation in the Auction(s).

It may be noted that Phase III policy has limited the number of private FM channels that may come up in a city. Accordingly, A+ cities have the ceiling of 9 to 11, A category cities 6, B category cities 4, C category cities 4, and D category cities 3.

It is heartening to note that 86 cities have been covered by FM radio services in Phase I and II. With the inclusion of 294 cities in Phase III, the total number of cities covered in all three phases is expected to reach 380.

Highlights of Phase III Policy: 2013

The important aspects of Phase III policy may be analyzed likewise.

- The existing Phase II operators will be allowed to migrate from Phase II to Phase III. The migration fee will be decided after consultation with telecom regulator TRAI for auction of 3G and broadband wireless access spectrum.

- To improve the viability further as against a maximum of 4 channels in D category cities (prescribed in FM Phase II), the new policy has proposed only 3 FM channels in D category cities. This would reduce fight for limited advertising revenue in a city.
- Phase III policy has limited the number of private FM channels that may come up in a city. Accordingly, A+ cities have the ceiling of 9 to 11, A category cities 6, B category cities 4, C category cities 4, and D category cities 3.
- In Phase III, the lock in period of shareholding of promoters/majority shareholders will be reduced from the present 5 years to 3 years. This would give the operators greater freedom to change the shareholding pattern.
- In Phase III, the license will be given to a private FM operator for 15 years as against 10 years in Phase II.
- Phase III policy would allow operators to distinguish themselves from others enabling them to cater to niche audiences. This would happen because of content diversification in view of news content, and also because of the provision of multiple-ownership of channels in a city, with the exception of D category cities. This would also increase the overall listenership base and the listening time.
- The additional channels that may become available due to a reduction in the inter-channel spacing to 400 KHz from the existing 800 KHz could be considered subsequently, after feasibility studies are undertaken in this regard.

Latest developments in Phase III Policy: 2015

Though Phase III policy of private FM radio was finalized in 2013, it could not take off since the rules regarding migration from Phase II to Phase III remained unresolved. So, the government handed over the issue to TRAI which submitted its recommendations by the end of 2014. The government did not lose any time in approving the TRAI recommendations, and notified the policy in January 2015.

Transparent SMRA E-Auction Methodology

The government, in fact, started preparations for allocating FM Phase III channels in 2014 only. The first step was the appointment of an Independent External Monitor in consultation with the Central Vigilance Commission to oversee the entire process of FM Phase III roll out including the e-auctions. Through global bidding, M/s C1 India Private Limited was selected by the government as independent external agency for e-auction of FM Phase III.

The Simultaneous Multiple Round Ascending (SMRA) e-Auction methodology has been adopted for FM Phase III licensing. This is the same model which is being used by the Department of Telecommunications for its spectrum auctions since 2010.

Bidding Process in Motion in 2015

The process of bidding started in the beginning of 2016. The government issued the Information Memorandum (IM) on January 21, 2015, as per Cabinet approval of January 16, 2015, for the first batch of 135 channels in 69 cities under Phase III. Following this, a pre-bid conference was held with all stakeholders in New Delhi, on January 28, 2015. The government received 85 queries and suggestion in this pre-bid and all queries were duly replied on February 17, 2015.

For the bidding process, the government also accepted some of industry's suggestions, prominent among them being the display of aggregate and excess demand, auction closure rule as per DOT's auctions, relaxation in cut-off date for determining the net worth of an applicant Company, identification of all possible frequencies for 135 channels.

The government then issued the Notice Inviting Applications (NIA) after incorporating suggestions accepted on IM for bidding for the first batch on March 2, 2015, which was followed by another pre bid conference with prospective bidders on March 10, 2015. The government received 76 queries in this conference and again all queries were duly replied, followed by an amendment to NIA on March 20, 2015.

After receiving 28 applications by the cut-off date of March 27, 2015 (5 PM), the government published the ownership details of all the applicants, which the bidders complied with. To create awareness among the bidders, the government conducted a training session on April 22, 2015 which was attended by all stakeholders. An Application Review Committee (ARC) appointed by the Government with representatives from Ministry of Law, Corporate Affairs, Finance, and Communications and IT, examined all the 28 applications.

After releasing list of pre-qualified bidders and including bidders as per the orders of Madras and Delhi High Courts, there remained 26 applicants for the first batch of FM Phase III. The government conducted another training session on July 17, 2015 with all the eligible bidders. This was followed by mock auctions for three days from July 22 to 24, 2015, to familiarize bidders with the rules and methodology for Phase III.

The e-Auction for the first batch of Phase III channels began on July 27, 2015. Four rounds of bidding were held daily and by August 14, 2015 which was the 15th day of bidding, 60 Rounds were completed. At the close of the 15th day of bidding, 91 channels in 56 cities became provisional winning channels with cumulative provisional winning price of about Rs 1079 Crore against their aggregate reserve price of about Rs 449 Crore. The total reserve price of the first batch of 135 channels was Rs 550.18 Crore.

Formal Beginning of Phase III Regime

The first batch auction marked the beginning of FM Phase III regime, which will bestow many new facilities on the operators under the regime. New regime also gives an operator facility to network its own channels within the country. Phase III regime permits the operators to carry the news bulletins of All India Radio in unaltered form on mutually agreed terms and conditions with Prasar Bharati.

As the government has revitalized its approach towards North Eastern part of India with its 'Act East' policy, FM Phase III policy projects this sentiment. It provides much needed support to the FM radio broadcasting services in cities of North Eastern part of India as in the cities of Jammu & Kashmir and Island territories, with provision of annual fee of the channels in these areas at half the rates for first three years, besides Prasar Bharti Infrastructure at half the lease rentals.

Phase III regime: Second batch auctions in 2016 and 2017

The much-awaited second batch of auctions of private FM Radio Phase III started in October 2016 and continued till February 2017. In the latest round, 266 FM channels were up for grabs in 92 cities. Initially, 58 channels in 42 cities were declared provisional winners. At the end of the auction, 66 frequencies were allotted across 48 cities.

Radio Mirchi won 21 frequencies while Red FM won 13. Red FM claims to be the highest spender during the auctions, pumping in Rs 80 crore for its frequencies. Radio City, Radio One and Big FM didn't participate in the auctions as they were content with the frequencies they won in the first batch of the auctions. However, Radio Mirchi and Red FM took part and won frequencies too.

Radio Mirchi, part of Entertainment Network India Limited (ENIL), won 21 frequencies. The player bagged frequencies in Akola, Amravati, Asansol, Bhavnagar, Durg-Bhillainagar and Hublli-Dhaward among other cities. Sun

Group's Kal Radio and South Asia FM too bagged a total of 13 frequencies. Kal Radio bagged six while South Asia FM bagged seven. The radio stations operate under the brand name Red FM. Kal Radio bagged frequencies in Erode, Hubli-Dharwad, Hyderabad, Nellore, Salem and Vellore while South Asia FM bagged frequencies in Agartala, Dehradun, Dhule, Jhansi, Leh, Muzaffarpur and Nanded.

Analysis of Private FM Radio Phase III Policy

The Phase III of private FM radio is said to be an important milestone in government's attempt to clock revenue as well as create entertainment and employment opportunities in several small cities of the country. These FM channels are expected to open doors of opportunity to the young regional talent spread across hundreds of cites in India.

The real success of Phase III of private FM broadcasting can be assessed only after these new channels roll out and start rendering their services to the listeners. However, the thrust of the policy, the initiatives taken and the process adopted for the formulation of the policy, and implementation on the policy, particularly the initial steps taken for putting the Phase III in motion can be analyzed as part of this study.

Assessment of Success of Phase III Policy

1. In Phase III, the process of e-auction is being adopted for the allotment of channels to prospective radio broadcasting operators. The bidding for the first and the second batches has taken place in a transparent manner which has been appreciated by one and all including the industry leaders.
2. In Phase III, private FM radio operators are expected to use distinct content so as to cater to niche audience. The content diversification may happen in view of news content, and also because of the provision of multiple-ownership of channels in a city, with the exception of D category cities. This is expected to

increase the overall listenership base and the listening time.

3. In Phase III, the lock in period of shareholding of promoters/majority shareholders has been reduced from the earlier cap of 5 years to 3 years. This would give private FM operators more freedom to change the shareholding pattern, thus, enhancing the viability of the business.

Phase III policy permits private FM radio operators (who had been given license under Phase II) to migrate from the old regime to the new regime. This is expected to facilitate existing private FM companies in sustenance and fill up large number of vacancies of FM channels.

Private FM Radio Policy in India: Contemporary Scenario

Seventeen years of Private FM Radio broadcasting in India has seen many ups and down. The merits and demerits of policies at any given time and the progress made over the years has been finally summed up in this study.

Analysing Policy Developments Till Date

1. Right from the beginning, the thrust of private FM broadcasting policy has been to take this powerful medium to every corner of the country. That is why Phase III has focused on D category cities, having population of more than one lakh and up to three lakh, while allocating licenses to radio operators.
2. The Private FM broadcasting policy marked the shift from rural to urban, as the thrust of this policy has been to develop radio as the medium of urban populace. This city centric broadcasting covered A+ and A category cities in Phase I (2000), B and C category cities in Phase II (2005) and D category cities in Phase III.
3. Right from the beginning, the government was contemplating of earning revenue by privatizing the FM broadcasting, but that did not happen. The

working group on Information and Broadcasting sector under Tenth Five Year Plan (2002-2007) found such a move counterproductive as it hindered the growth of FM services in the first phase.

So, the government had to take corrective policy measures in Phase II so as to make the policy pragmatic and friendly to entrepreneurs. This helped the government in fetching huge sums in the second and the third phase. In the first and the second batches of Phase III bidding, the government has succeeded in collecting huge sums as license fees.

4. The thrust of the policy has been on providing healthy entertainment to listeners. For making sure that the entertainment remains healthy, legal and ethical guidelines have been prescribed for FM operators. The private FM radio channels have opened new doors for young talent, and have generated numerous employment opportunities. However, no data is available on this aspect.
5. Phase I and II policies of private FM radio was confined to entertainment only, but Phase III has a thrust on information also. The Phase I and Phase II policies did not allow the broadcast of news, but Phase III policy has corrected this with conditions attached. Now, the FM operators can carry AIR news bulletins though they are not allowed to produce and broadcast their own news bulletin. The line between news and non-news, which was blurred in Phase I and II, has also been drawn clearly in Phase III policy.
6. To keep a check on monopolies in the broadcasting sector, the limit on the ownership of channels, at the national level, allocated to an entity is retained at 15 percent in the Phase III, similar to the cap prescribed in Phase II. The city wise limit of owning the channels has been modified in Phase III. Private operators are allowed to own more than one channel but not more

than 40 percent of the total channels in a city subject to a minimum of three different operators in the city.

7. To enable private broadcasters generating enough capital to run the show, Phase III policy has allowed the total direct and indirect foreign investment including portfolio and foreign direct investment in a FM broadcast company to the tune of 26 % (at the time of application and during the currency of the license). In Phase II, this limit was 20 %.
8. The policymakers have been striving hard to maintain a balance between the interest of private FM operators of networking their channels and the interest of listeners of getting local content from a radio channel. In Phase II policy, a private FM operator was allowed to network its own channels only in C and D categories cities of a region. The Phase III policy permits the networking of channels within a FM broadcaster's own network across the country. However, no two entities are permitted to network any of their channels in any category of cities.

To ensure purity of local content, Phase III policy stipulates that at least 20% of the total broadcast in a day (reckoned from 0000 Hrs to 2400 Hrs), is in the local language of that city and promotes local content. This may include the Radio Jockey speaking in local language(s)/dialect(s) or programmes focused on local culture/tradition/folk music etc. or other permissible programmes/advertisements in the local language(s)/dialect(s).

Assessment of Process Adopted for Formulation of Policies

1. The private FM radio policy was formulated for the first time by the government in July 1999, but it was full of flaws. So, the government set up a committee for suggesting improvement in the policy in 2003. In January 2004, the government issued a notification appointing TRAI a policy consultant for broadcasting, and the report of the committee was handed over to

TRAI. Since then, TRAI continues to be a consultant and Phase II and Phase III policies have been formulated in consultation with TRAI.

2. In the formulation of Phase III policy, the GOM and EGOM also contributed significantly. But this has simply delayed the process of policy formulation. The Phase III policy which could have been put in place in 2009 delayed since the GOM gave its report in 2011and EGOM gave its report in 2013. Again, the government sought the help of TRAI on the issue of migration, and the policy could be finalized only in 2014.

Evaluating Success Rate and Future Prospect

1. In Phase I of private FM radio policy, only 21 channels in 12 cities could become operational; and the success rate was only 25%. Following completion of bidding for Phase II in 2007, only 136 channels (including Phase I channels) could become operational. By the end of Ninth FYP (1997-2002), only 30 % population of the country could be covered by private FM radio channels. The Tenth FYP (2002-2007) set a target of raising the coverage from 30 % 60 %, but only 40 % could be achieved by 2007.
2. The government continued bidding for filling up the vacancies, and 185 radio stations came into operation in 92 cities by the end of 2012. However, auction for 97 channels could not take place for various reasons in Phase II. The Eleventh FYP (2007-2012) set a target of raising the coverage from 40 % to 75 %, but only 60 % could be achieved by 2012.
3. The government has decided to set up 839 private FM radio channels in 294 cities in Phase III, but the process is very slow. The bidding process was completed for 135 channels in 69 cities for the first batch of the allotment of channels in August 2015. In the second batch, bidding process for 227 channels in 69 cities was completed in February 2017.

4. With the existing pace, Phase III licensing may take 8 to 10 years. It is only after the completion of Phase III, the coverage may reach 80 % of the population.

To sum up

Private FM radio broadcasting has now entered into a new era where many things are happening for the first time. The most important factor is the coverage across the country. The States of Uttarakhand and Nagaland, and the Border Area Towns of Poonch, Mokukchung, Leh, Kathua, Kargil and Bhaderwa will have private FM channels for the first time. The cities of Agartala and Aizawl will also have FM radio stations.

Many big radio broadcasting companies have emerged bigger after Phase III auction. For instance, Radio Mirchi now has 71 channels in 64 cities. Red FM has also succeeded in establishing its presence in most of the state capitals with consolidation in Hindi speaking territories of the country. The expansion has to be welcomed, though the concentration of companies raises questions about media monopolies and cross-media ownership.

Despite fierce bidding and the success of the government in collecting huge amounts through licensing, the issue of viability of radio business in smaller towns is looming large on the growth of Private FM radio broadcasting. Radio operators must be ready to face the music; or the government might be showing wisdom by amending the policy.

3

Who is the Community in Community Radio?

Dr. Savita Bailur

Despite the enthusiasm for community-owned radio, a movement which has been steadily gaining pace since the implementation of new legislation of 2006, we are yet to find an understanding of who the community is in community radio. Through an extended case study, this analysis shows how "community participation" is constantly shifting. It presents three arguments: "community" is not a discrete entity; communities are dynamic; and communities are cognitive constructs.

Following the decision of the Supreme Court in 1996 that the "airwaves are public property", and the implementation of new guidelines for non-governmental organisation (NGO)-owned community radio in November 2006, the movement for community radio has been rapidly gaining momentum in India. In 2011, it was estimated that 82 community radios were operational in India, with a further 121 having signed the "grant of permission agreement" with the Ministry of Information and Broadcasting. It is frequently stated that

---

Dr. Savita Bailur (S.bailur@lse.ac.uk) is a research associate at the London School of Economics, London.

community radio is the most relevant form of media for socially excluded groups, due to its lower technological cost (both of the station and receiver sets), low literacy levels required, and therefore, relatively low barriers to entry and participation (Girard 1992; Gumucio Dagron 2001; Noronha 2003; Pavarala 2003a; Gumucio Dagron and Tufte 2006).

For these reasons, community radio is considered a critical medium for development and social change (Melkote and Steeves 2001; Noronha 2003; Tacchi 2005; Gumucio Dagron and Tufte 2006; Pavarala and Malik 2007). The unfailing emphasis is that for community radio to be relevant, contextual and sustainable, it must be owned by the "community" (Pavarala and Malik 2007). Undoubtedly, one of the key challenges to this is that completely community-owned radio is still non-existent in India, as a Letter of Intent to the Ministryof Information and Broadcasting has to be issued by educational institutions or NGOs. A second challenge is one that we argue here is little discussed in community radio literature in India. Namely, who constitutes the community in community radio and how exactly does community participation occur?

Based on eight consecutive months of fieldwork in 2006, and return visits in the ensuing three years, this paper deconstructs how community is formed and unformed, and participationis equally fluid in a donor-established community radio station, which we will anonymise here as "Avaaz". It isargued that more acknowledgement needs to be made that community is not a discrete entity, that communities, and therefore, participation are dynamic, and finally, that communities are cognitive and performed. First, a brief overview is given of how community is seen in community radio. This is posited against the broader discussion and deconstruction of community both in sociology and development. Our three theoretical arguments are then presented. The case of Avaaz and the methodology used to research it are introduced next. Finally, we provide examples to substantiate our theoretical stance on community, and provide relevant conclusions and recommendations.

1. An Overview

1.1 The 'Community' in Community Radio

Numerous authors write that only community participation and ownership will lead to relevant programming, sustainability of community radio and empowerment of the local community (Girard 1992; Gumucio Dagron 2001; Tacchi 2003; Tacchi 2005; Lewis and Jones 2006; Fuller 2007; Pavarala and Malik 2007). AMARC (the French acronym for the World Association of Community Radio) defines community radio itself as "a non-profit station, currently broadcasting, which offers a service to the community in which it is located, or to which it broadcasts, while promoting the participation of this community in the radio". Fuller (2007) states that ownership and control of community media is rooted in and responsible to the communities they serve. Rodrigues states that "empowerment, conscientisation and fragmentation of power result when the men, women and youth gain access to and reclaim their own media" (cited by Tacchi 2005). According to Pavarala and Malik (2007) "community radio helps to put the community members in charge of their own affairs" (ibid: 18). Gumucio Dagron states that community radio "has to think locally first in order to consolidate cultural identity and reflect needs" (2007: 206).

Pavarala (2003b) is one of the few to provide a detailed case study on a community radio in India (Chala Ho Gaon Mein), but concludes ...conscious efforts should be made by all the community reporters to involve as many villagers as possible in programme production as it has been observed that those villages which have contributed to programme content also tend to be more committed audiences (p 2197).

There is an emphasis on preservation of local language, culture and identity (Gumucio Dagron 2007). Volunteers with dedication (Dunaway 2002) and collective community ownership (Salazar 2007) are called for. Pasha states that "a localradio station must be flexible and spontaneous to enable itself to function as the mouthpiece of the local community"

(1997: 12). There is a particular emphasis for marginalised groups such as women and tribal groups to use community radio to give them a voice (Pavarala and Malik 2007; Aleaz 2010). Yet, within such statements lie several challenges: what (or who) is the community in community radio? Pavarala (2003a) defines community as "a territorially bound group with some commonality of interest" (p 2166). What is local language, culture and identity, as called for by Gumucio Dagron? Is collective community ownership ever possible? What are the processes by which a local radio station comes to function as the mouthpiece of the local community? In other words, what are power struggles in the community in enacting community participation? As Hoccheimer (1993:473-86) asks, "who serves whom? Who speaks for which community interest? Who decides what are the legitimate voices to be heard?" (ibid: 480).

1.2 Debates on Community and Community Participation

Participation in community radio is specifially seen as "activities related to involving people directly in station programming, administration and policy activities" (Prehn 1991: 259). In theory, community radio listeners are the producers, managers, directors and even owners of stations (Girard 1992: 2). As seen above, there is a tendency to view community media as owned by a holistic community. However, in the fields of sociology and development, it is argued that community is a symbolic construction rather than a given (Cohen 1985; Cleaver 2001; Cooke and Kothari 2001). Some state that the homogenisation is a form of government surveillance and control from colonial times when community was a constructed "other" to be governed (Dar and Cooke 2008). It is argued that this holistic entity conceals discrete interest groups and power dynamics such as race, religion, class, caste and gender (Gujit and Shah 1998; Botchway 2001; Cleaver 2001; Mosse 2001). Authors caution that emphasis on community participation, local empowerment and building social capital underplays local inequalities and power relations. It is also stated that in light of caste and class hierarchies in south Asian cultures, community is a particularly complicated, and perhaps unachievable, entity (Tharoor 2000; Jodhka 2001).

Sociological debates also critique the notion of a holistic culture or identity. It is argued that one's affinity to culture is relational (Featherstone 1995), while Tajfel and Turner (1979) have spoken of social identity theory, where culture is iteratively and dynamically performed against shifting reference points, including ethnicity and religion. Therefore, it is accepted that a constructivist notion of community and local culture may provide a useful shorthand, but is reductionist and static (Sihlongonyane 2009), particularly in today's globalised, dynamic "scapes" (Appadurai 1990). One may speak of the "Muslim community of Bangalore", but within this created, holistic "Muslim community", there will be further networks dependent on neighbourhoods resided in, friendships made, schools and universities attended, and so on. In short, a geographically bounded community may exist but comprises other multifarious networks.

Admittedly, there is some acknowledgement of these fractures and frictions within community, and therefore, "community participation" in community media literature. Pavarala and Malik (2007) note that there needs to be further understanding of what this term means. It has been argued that because of the connotations of a holistic community in community radio, other terms should be used such as "alternative radio" or "citizens' radio" (Lewis 1993; Tacchi 2003; Fuller 2007). Challenges in community participation in community radio have been documented, for example, attempts at appropriation by pentecostal and evangelical churches on community radio in Guatemala and Bolivia (Gumucio Dagron 2007) or between different groups of women in a female community radio in the United Kingdom, as opposed to treating "women" as a holistic group which need to be empowered (Mitchell 2002), or local politicians trying to use a UNESCO-supported community radio in Benin as their propaganda machine, having donated to it (Dlamini 2004).

Instead of community media reflecting a holistic, specific, local culture then, it is more likely to fit in with Appadurai's (1990) conceptualisation of a dynamic, global "mediascape" (Jayaprakash and Shoesmith 2007).

Similarly, it is not a given that community media should only discuss local issues - in their research, Jayaprakash and Shoesmith (ibid) find that listeners and producers of Ooty Radio Station are not interested in representing "local culture", for example, programmes of local methods of agricultural production because "if it is local, it is not new" (p 49).

Therefore, we put forward three theoretical elements here: first, community is not a discrete, holistic entity which will uniformly "participate" in community radio; second, communities are dynamic, and finally, communities are cognitive and performed entities. These arguments may seem self-evident, but it is believed that they are insufficiently discussed in discussion groups or policies in India, or even in community radio literature (including in past papers in this journal) where community radio is largely seen as a panacea for communities deprived of "voice", in a battle against the Ministry of Information and Broadcasting or mass media. In the following sections, we first deconstruct these three theoretical elements, before applying the case of Avaaz.

1.3 Community is Not a Discrete Entity

It has been argued that although an attractive proposition, community is not a discrete entity (Cohen 1985; Cleaver 2001; Cooke and Kothari 2001; Sihlongonyane 2009). Instead, it is more useful to turn towards how social relationships are formed within and through networks (Wellman 1983; Wellman and Berkowitz 1988; Kilduff and Tsai 2003; Marin and Wellman 2010). Actors in networks are bound together through homophily, that is the interaction with others who share similar goals and values to themselves, which itself is a subjectively interpreted criteria (Louch 2000; McPherson et al 2001). Therefore, we seek to belong to networks where we feel our interests will be served. We may even adhere to long defunct values in the desire to belong to networks (Emirbayer and Goodwin 1994) and avoid ostracisation. However, because different networks bring us different benefits, we also belong to multiple networks, and this multiple network belonging may result in conflict when the goals of different networks clash, and one goal is more important than another (Human and Provan 2000). We may belong to a community then, but multiple spider webs of relations exist within this overall grouping.

1.4 Communities are Dynamic

As we belong to multiple networks, the argument follows that this network belonging is always dynamic. Menjívar illustrates how networks of immigrants from El Salvador in the United States are welcoming to new immigrants, but shrink during times of financial crisis (Menjívar 2000). Kapferer (1972) analyses how at times of strike action in an Indian owned textile factory in Zambia, network allegiances shift, according to who the workers think is more important. Zachary documented goal conflict in a karate club, where the club president and club instructor disagreed over the price and type of karate offered, subsequently dividing the club (Zachary 1977). Similarly, Chatterjee (1998) shows how what appears to be a cohesive community in a Kolkata slum is constructed of multiple networks based on actors' self concerns and awareness of repercussions on themselves. The consequence of belonging to multiple networks then is that we are always assessing which networks bring us more value. Therefore, in terms of participation, this will also always be dynamic as actors reassess which networks they belong to, which bring value to them and whether it is worth participating or not.

1.5 Communities are Cognitive

Finally, we argue that communities are not static, objective entities because they, like all relationships, are mental constructs. This is illustrated by an example given by Cialdini of the financier Baron De Rothschild when petitioned for a loan by an acquaintance, who replied to the latter: "I won't give you a loan myself... I will walk arm in arm with you across the floor of the stock exchange and you will soon have willing lenders to spare" (1989: 45). Simply the association of being with Rothschild is considered enough to make others think that the potential borrower is trustworthy. A network is temporary and ephemeral because according to Strathern, it is no more than "the tracery of heterogenous elements...or string of circumstances, held by social interactions...in short a hybrid imagined in a socially extended state" (1996: 521). A network is temporary because events may occur which weaken or strengthen it, as illustrated by Kapferer (1972). It is also temporary because it is subjective, as network construction is the result of individual cognitive maps (Weick and Bougon 1986).

Network membership may not only be constructed on the basis of which networks, individuals feel they belong to, but also which they feel they do not belong to. A famous example of this is given by Gino and Ayal (2009) in a controlled experiment where students cheated more when they saw those from their own university cheating, but not when they saw those from a rival university cheating (because they felt they were above the rival university and did not follow these values). This is linked to ideas of how we perform in different social contexts, as discussed by the American sociologist Erving Goffman (1959). The next section introduces the case of Avaaz before analysing it through these three constructs: communities as networks, communities as dynamic entities, and communities as cognitive and performed constructs.

2. The Case of Avaaz

The case of Avaaz has been anonymised here in order to protect those who were working there at the time, although it is understood that first, it may still be recognisable from the few details given, and second, a weakness of the anonymisation is that much detail has been lost. This raises larger questions of research ethics (protecting research subjects) (Dodson and Sterling 2010) versus reliability (Hammersley 1992). These are complex issues which deserve further discussion on living research subjects such as contemporary community media (Sterling and Rangaswamy 2010), but are beyond the scope of this paper.

Avaaz is a community radio which was already narrowcasting through NGOs in 2001, when it was given support from adonor agency in 2002. This support included a new studio, as well as four computers for IT teaching, a printer, photocopier and scanner. There was also in theory an internet connection for radio browsing, a technique previously employed in Kothmale Community Radio in Sri Lanka, where the DJ could look up information online and broadcast it over the radio (Noronha 2003), but it is unclear whether this ever worked at Avaaz. Two NGOs were involved in assisting the operationalisation of Avaaz, made anonymous here as Jaan (a development NGO) and Maatu (a media NGO). The main aim of Avaaz was to combine new and traditional technologies to produce relevant local content, in local languages to improve the quality of life for people in rural communities, especially in poorer households. In order to be sustainable, Avaaz solicited support from already existing local self-help groups (SHGs) as well as the local panchayat, and it was located in an accessible area next to the village bus stop. The management committee comprised representatives from the SHGs, and staff and volunteers were recruited from the local catchment. All the latter were intended to participate in programme design, content, production, management and evaluation of Avaaz.

2.1 Research Methodology

An overall extended case study approach (Burawoy 2009) was pursued while researching Avaaz. This involved a pilot visit in 2004, eight consecutive months at Avaaz in 2006, and subsequent brief research trips in 2007, 2008 and 2009. Interpreters were used in this period, because while I had a basic understanding of the local language, I was not fluent in it. Interviews recounted here are with Guru (the centre manager, employed by Jaan), Shivani (the ex-project manager, employed by Maatu and the donor), Ramesh (the subsequent project manager, employed by Maatu), and past and present staff and volunteers.

One specific analytical method was that of narrative analysis. This refrains from treating interviews as hard data, and instead sees the storytelling itself as revealing in how interviewees see themselves and others (Riessman 1993; Czarniawska-Joerges 1998). In narrative analysis, what is critical is the construction of the plot (defined as an original state of affairs, an action/event, and a consequent state of affairs or resolution) (Riessman 1993; Boje 2001). Who includes what and who omits what (a process Riessman calls selectivity). How does the passage of time influence the story (Ricoeur 1988; Levine 1997; Cunliffe et al 2004)? What is a storyteller's "cognitive resolution" (Chafe 1990) as to why something happened, and what their role was in the story? Therefore, in what way does the story result in the storyteller's self making (Bruner 2003)? For these reasons, narrative analysis complements the perspective of performance and cognitive constructs of community, as we see how interviewees use the relevant "social dialect" (Casey 1993) depending on how they see themselves, the circumstances in which they narrate their story (where the interview takes place, who else is present, how soon after the event it takes place as time itself is a subjective entity and cognitive resolution may have occurred in that intervening time, the relationship between interviewer, interpreter and interviewee, etc.) and how they wish to be perceived.

2.2 Networks of Participation in Avaaz

As mentioned above, Avaaz illustrated community participation by not only recruiting studio managers and volunteer staff from the village in which it was based, but also by establishing a management committee drawing from the 12 SHGs in the village. In network terminology, it could be said that this network was "goal directed" (Kilduff and Tsai

2003) with a common goal of creating a community radio constituting local content represented by local people. Shivani, an early project manager, emphasised the "access to all" mantra which made Avaaz "a casteless, genderless place". However, this goal directed network on establishing Avaaz overlaid existing networks of religion, caste and family feuds. Shivani illustrated this with an example of religion: "I did play devil's advocate and said if you want to play a prayer song, does it have to be a Hindu song every day? What about the Muslim community? And they said no, the Muslim community can come in and sing their song every Friday... this was the time of the whole Babri masjid event, there was a lot of tension". It is seen therefore how the opening prayer song is heavily influenced by religious allegiances, and there is no one holistic community, but rather a division into the Hindu and Muslim community (and the "spokeswomen" for the "Hindu community" create a holistic "the Muslim community" as it serves to justify their decision, a point which we will return to in discussing how communities are cognitive). Similarly, when Bhavana, one of the volunteers, was asked of her time at the station, and if there were any issues of caste, gender or religion, she replied "nothing like that, even the backward castes used to come, they used to mingle with us". Narratively, her inclusion of "*even the backward castes*" implies an extension to these castes which is not usual. The distinction "*they used to mingle with us*" illustrates an underlying delineation of "them" and "us".

The argument that a "goal directed" network of Avaaz overlaid existing networks was also illustrated by the example of Sheila, another Avaaz staff member in 2006. In early interviews, Sheila had stated that "giving awareness is important. Information is important. It is good to help others". Yet, later in fieldwork, still in 2006, she came subdued to work one day. Her elder sister had been suffering a difficult pregnancy and on birth, it was discovered that the baby's oesophagus and trachea were fused. She said "we talk about information on health, we are the ones who keep telling other people to listen. But none of this is worth anything if you don't have money". Sheila's comments and cognitive resolution showed how her very real family challenges affected on how much she believed the value of her work.

Finally, the idea that participation in Avaaz (particularly on programmes raising awareness about corruption or local middlemen) was influenced by actors' membership of other networks was made by Guru, the centre manager: "poorer people do not want to get involved. Because supposing they complain about the richer people, and later the richer people offer work, they will not support them if they have complained before". Even though, according to Ramesh, the Maatu project manager, attempts were made to preserve anonymity such as polls and vox pops, people were reluctant to participate in such programmes for fear of repercussions (Emirbayer and Goodwin 1994; Chatterjee 1998), unless it was already clear they did not belong to these.

2.3 Dynamic Networks in Avaaz

It is, of course, understandable that between 2001, when the centre is said to have started, and 2006 (the start of our research), participation in Avaaz had morphed continuously. As illustrated by Kapferer (1972), Menjívar (2000) and Zachary (1977), network membership changes because of seminal moments. This was also the case in Avaaz. One event recounted by Shivani was that of a volunteers strike as a result of one of the SHG members storming into the centre to demand the broadcast of her as yet unedited programme. The volunteers found the episode disturbing, and went on strike until their respect and security was assured. However, in an illustration of the influence of time over narrative (Levine 1997), Ricoeur's fiction effect (Ricoeur 1988) and Riessman's selectivity (1993), it is notable that none of the volunteers mentioned this when interviewed.

A second seminal event in Avaaz was the theft of a digital camera by one of the volunteers. According to Shivani and Guru, the event was not considered particularly relevant, but the panchayat was insistent on punishment and the two boys implicated were held overnight in a cell. The camera was recovered in bushes nearby. Again, the actual circumstances surrounding this were never clear as varying narratives were told. According to Shivani, "next day, a group of 20 or so volunteers came to the centre. They said we will never volunteer for you again, and we will make sure nobody in this village ever volunteers for you again". Again, selectivity emerged when interviewed in 2006, most of the volunteers who were there at the time did not mention this. Only one, Anand, stated that "there had been some problem with Nikhil and Kamal and after that, people began leaving... when people left no one else went and the centre became quiet" (although note, the explicit mention of the theft was omitted).

However, one strong account came from Arun, a volunteer and subsequent studio manager at the time of the theft. According to him "after the camera was found, the person who stole it was reappointed. I was disappointed .... [H]e had robbed, and if he served in [Avaaz], others will learn to rob. As long as he is there, I will not go back there. We kept asking the management committee not to employ him, but they did".

Arun's narrative thus illustrates a moving away from the goal directed network of Avaaz workers. He added "all the good people left at this time, first Suresh, then Divya, then Rajendra, then me... we kept asking the management committee not to employ Nikhil, but they did". The composition of the narrative illustrates his self-making (Bruner 2003): by distancing himself from the person who committed this theft, and including himself as one of "all the good people", he shows himself as someone who no longer wished to belong to the network of Avaaz. Instead, his focus on the camera theft as a primary experience (Riessman 1993), illustrates how he uses it to place himself along with Suresh, Divya and Rajendra in the smaller network, bound by more honourable ties and stronger values against theft, against the larger network of the management committee and Nikhil.

The third seminal event, the departure of Divya, again illustrates the fracturing and changing networks of participation in community radio. Once again, the actual circumstances are not clear, due to conflicting accounts. According to Shivani, Divya wanted to leave for a higher paid job, but unable to do so, she decided to withdraw her resignation. When this was not approved, Shivani remembers that Divya began "mobilising opinions against the radio station... it came to the point where the MC [management committee] were seeing it as Guru and Shivani versus her, and they were on her side". Once more, this suggests that networks were fracturing, cliques forming, and where once an overall network working on Avaaz was constructed, now the radio station was being seen as Guru and Shivani versus Divya and the management committee. If the representatives of the MC were meant to be from the community, if they saw the radio station as "being seen as Guru and Shivani", then this would illustrate a lack of community participation (although it should be remembered that this was Shivani's own narrative: once more, the MC members interviewed were silent on this matter, except that "Guru is not from here" and therefore did not understand the village).

The fourth seminal event which again appeared to divide networks and therefore participation was the live recording of the village gram sabha which was played on the radio. At the start of the establishment of Avaaz, Ramesh from Maatu stated that "it was one of the villages where the panchayat willingly said, okay, you can take the building, you don't have to pay rent, and the people were very excited". According to him, one of the early ideas was "like fertilisers are being given for free, or a special fertiliser is being given, we broadcast that information. Something government is giving out, something that these guys don't know about and we are the link". The use of the phrase "we are the link" is particularly inoffensive, and so the idea of working together rather than against (i.e., belonging to the same network). However, in 2002, when the annual gram sabha meeting was recorded live, "the panchayat had a big fight" (Guru). Further events caused further fractures: an annual Jamma Bundi which again the radio station raised awareness about, but the panchayat "changed the date and they did not tell us" (Guru), and the 2005 live broadcast of local elections. According to Guru "we go from Avaaz and they openly say, every Prime Minister is corrupt, every chief minister is corrupt, why do you want to talk about us only?".

Therefore, although initially Ramesh perceived homophily (Louch 2000; McPherson et al 2001), it is clear this is no longer the case (according to Guru and the panchayat), and in fact, the latter feels victimised as they are only part of a larger corrupt system.

Other critical events occurred during fieldwork in 2006. Through August and September 2006, the only live Avaaz broadcasts were to the outlying Ambedkar colonies, where loudspeakers had been placed. One evening in late September, a young boy mentioned that "somebody had the cables". One of the loudspeakers was also missing. Later that evening, celebrations for the Ganesh Chaturthi festival began in the village. A pick-up truck with a loudspeaker system paraded through the local area, accompanied by much festivity. Rumours began circulating that it was the same loudspeaker which had been stolen. When asked if this was the case, one of the revellers jokingly replied "it is ours only" playing on the concept of ownership and therefore, their right to do whatever they wished with the equipment. In contrast, when Guru brought up this issue many months later, he complained "it is not their property to do that": a marked deviation from the original rhetoric of community participation and ownership.

One final event involved Rani, one of the Avaaz staff, who was being harassed by a young boy calling her daily at the station during fieldwork. After one call, she decided to go home for the day. Her father visited in the afternoon, stating that it was no place for young women, and that Rani would be leaving. Although Rani had until now somewhat successfully negotiated multiple network belonging, two of which were the family network and work network, the goals of these two clash (Human and Provan 2000; Kilduff and Tsai

2003) and it is no longer beneficial for her to be part of the work network. Thus, even though Ramesh had stated that one of the attempts to make the centre "community owned" was its location next to the bus stop and therefore "very, very accessible", despite the fact that we encountered Rani several times at the bus stop next to the centre, she did not re-enter the premises. This, and the above examples of the volunteers strike, camera theft, departure of Divya, division from the panchayat and loudspeaker theft lead us to the argument that community inclusion and exclusion is also a matter of perception, i.e., cognitive.

2.4 Cognitive Communities in Avaaz

In the above perspectives, it has been argued that communities comprise multiple networks, and are therefore, dynamic as an individual's aims might begin to differ from the aims of the network. However, changing network membership is not simply an action. In most cases, as argued above (Weick and Bougon 1986; Cialdini 1989; Strathern 1996; Gino and Ayal 2009), this network membership is cognitive and therefore, performed (Goffman 1959). Initially for example, most of the Avaaz workers saw themselves as distinct from the larger uneducated community. According to Guru "we are supporting the community... everything the community does". Sheila saw herself as "giving awareness" to "others". In 2004, Divya mentioned "the large difference between rural and urban people" and how "we are helping change that". "Giving awareness is important. Information is important... we tell others boil water nicely, keep your house clean". Yet, through the course of research, all three individuals showed their concerns about this goal-focused network of Avaaz. The baby's death illustrated this in the case of Sheila. For Divya, the turning point appeared to be when she attempted to leave. In 2004, she had placed herself in a benevolent, somewhat hierarchical position of helping others and educating the rural people to the level of the urban. However, in 2006, instead of standing apart from "the community" as she had done in 2004, she stated the reason she had been asked to leave was because she did not make "innovative programmes". She asked "what is innovative? I live in the village – how innovative can I be? I am a simple village girl". Thus, we can see how Divya cognitively changes positions, from outside the community, to inside it, and constructing herself as "a simple village girl" when it is helpful for her.

It is also interesting how community membership was frequently invoked to justify whether programme content was relevant or not. We saw it above when the Hindu community decides what a constructed "Muslim community" should do, even though crosscutting networks existed between these two "communities", e.g., the SHG members were also neighbours, had children who went to the same school, were babysitters for each other, etc. Similarly, Jagadish, the first IT teacher, complained that the original content was "blade, blade, blade [boring]... am also boring here are only. So I know how the community people like, I know". Even though Jagadish now lived in the state capital, he considered himself as belonging from there. In contrast, although Guru had lived and worked in the area for 11 years, it was often pointed out that "he was not from here" and therefore, did not understand the village, and therefore, political processes which affected participation (even though, as seen above, he had illustrated an understanding of why people were reluctant to speak out). Similarly, the acting panchayat president stated that "they only want to complain about us... nobody from that centre understands our village", even though all the volunteers and staff (including Guru, who lived behind the centre) lived in that village or outlying ones. Thus, even though in this case the panchayat and Avaaz staff geographically constituted the same community, the first half of the definition of community used by Pavarala (2003) ("a territorially bound group"), they did not, as seen in the research, represent a community in the second half of his definition ("with some commonality of interest"), as they did not perceive themselves as having the same goals. Yet again, in an illustration of how dynamic networks, and therefore communities, are, it was observed that in the preparations for a Republic Day parade in 2007, the panchayat and the centre worked together putting differences aside, because once more this was a common goal. Perhaps the individual who illustrated the greatest cognitive construction in and out of different networks was Guru. As seen above, he frequently distanced himself from the community, which he was merely supporting. Returning to discuss the retaining of Nikhil, he stated: "even Nikhil, I did not want to take back. Till this day, I oppose his inclusion, but community decided". This multiple network membership, however, was not without discomfort for him. His uncertainty and attempts at cognitive resolution emerged in his narrative with statements such as "we, that is they, Jaan", showing him unclear as to whether he belonged to Jaan or not. However, a visit by a Reliance mobile phone salesman (to use the centre as a sales point) also illustrated Guru's attempts to benefit from this multiple network membership, shown in the following conversation:

Reliance salesman: "What can we do for you, so that we can make this happen?" [For the centre to be an outlet for Reliance mobile phones.]

Guru: "Give me some money, we are so happy".
Reliance salesman: "That is there".
Guru: "Some incentive, anything, like 50 phones we sell, we get a motorbike."
[Guru and salesman laugh]
Guru: "I am thinking, I am helping, getting information, ICTs to the people. So 50 phones, one bike. 100 phones, one car."
Reliance salesman: "This will be a costly thing for us".
Guru: "We want people to get a connection, to get ICTs".
Reliance salesman: "So, it is not only upliftment of the community, it is also upliftment for you".
[Guru and salesman laugh]
Guru: "I am also community, no? I'm joking."

As seen, Guru first constructs himself as helping "the people" but when his "upliftment of the community" is gently mocked, he constructs themselves as part of the community, as it is more beneficial for him. This and the examples of the changing perceptions of Sheila, Divya, the panchayat, and how Arun chooses not to see himself as part of the Avaaz network after he believes it condones the camera theft (although note how Guru himself attributes this to the "community"), all illustrate how communities are dynamic because they are cognitive creations.

3. Discussion and Conclusions

It could justifiably be asked what the benefits are of such a somewhat theoretical discussion on what constitutes community in community radio. However, the main point of this paper is that there is an insufficient deconstruction of the complexities of community in community radio literature and discussion in India. Too often we see a binary distinction in community radio between an oppressive government or mass media and wholesome community radio (Pasha 1997; Mitchell and Baxter 2006). Instead, it should be understood that the processes of community participation in community radio are no different to any other participatory and democratic processes, in illustrating the cleavages, power struggles and temporary alliances which come together, but also disintegrate. For this reason, we can only emphasise the need for more detailed case studies on community radio in India, which are all too rare (see for a few examples, Aleaz (2010), Pavarala and Malik (2007) and Slater and Tacchi (2003)). An extended case method and narrative analysis were understandably a luxury of doctoral research, but if at all possible more thought needs to be given to qualitative and ethnographic style research in community media, where we listen to what people say, and therefore, their understandings of community and "participation".

Courtesy: April 28, 2012 vol xlviI no 17 , EPW Economic & Political Weekly

4

The World of Campus Community Radio

Dr. Chetna Bhatia

What is Campus Radio

Development of community radio in India witnessed a path breaking trend when Ministry of Information & Broadcasting, Government of India made a policy in December 2002 and invited educational institutions to set up community radio stations in their campuses or premises which would be run by them. Therefore, it is also called college radio or university radio or student radio. There is no given official definition of a 'Campus Radio', but it broadly refers to the radio station run by the students of a university or college. The essential features of such kind of radio stations include establishing its infrastructure inside the premises of that educational institution along with its program content and presentation being done majorly by the students studying there. For example, DUCR is run by the students of Delhi University, MICAVAANI is run by the students of Mudra Institute of Communications Ahmedabad from its premises.

Chetna Bhatia is Assistant Professor at VIPS (GGSIP University), New Delhi.

As per the guidelines of I&B Ministry which governs this process and grants license for it, campus radio is considered as a form of community radio. It also includes those stations which have been set up in different government schools. According to the government policy on community radio, following categories of institutions are allowed to set up and run community radio in India–

(*a*) Non-Government Organizations
(*b*) State Agricultural Universities
(*c*) Educational Institutions–Government
(*d*) Educational Institutions–Private
(*e*) Universities (including deemed to be universities)
(*f*) Krishi Vigyan Kendras

The scope of campus radio in India includes both government and private run educational institutions alongwith universities.

History of Campus Radio

Educational institutions of various countries had been running college radio or campus radio with different purposes and under different policies of their respective governments. According to Jennifer Waits (2010), *"much of college radio's history is unwritten and pinpointing the first or oldest college radio is a challenge."* However different countries have witnessed emergence of this powerful medium at different time periods in the history. The oldest Campus radio in US was 'WRUC Radio' that was established in 1920 at Union College Schenectady in New York. In United Kingdom, the first college radio known to be established was 'Crush Radio' at University of Hertfordshire in 1960. Further the wave touched Canada in 1975 with 'CKCU FM', Portugal in 1986 with Radio 'Universidad de Coimbra', Switzerland in 1993 with 'Frequence Banane', Australia in 1994 with 'UCFM' and more recently in Bangladesh with 'BUET Radio' in 2015.

In India, Anna FM made a landmark by setting up the first campus community radio station of the country on 1st

February 2004. It was followed by Radio Jamia at AJK Mass Communication Research Centre Jamia Millia Islamia University, Apna Radio at Indian Institute of Mass Communication, Delhi and MICAVAANI at Mudra Institute of Communications Ahmedabad in 2005. More recently, National Institute of Open Schooling (NIOS) launched its campus radio on 25th December 2015 to educate students by broadcasting the lectures delivered there for those who are out of school. It was followed by the launching of 'Radio Salesian' at Salesian College, Darjeeling (on 29th October 2016 and NIT Trichy on 23rd November 2016. As per the data released by Ministry of Information & Broadcasting on 1st November 2016, there are more than 200 community radio stations operating in India and 110 of them fall in the category of campus radio. A detailed list can be seen in the form of a table at the end of this chapter.

Students recording the programs at Radio Luit, Gauhati University, Assam

Source: The Mileage

Campus Radio vs. Other Forms of Community Radio

Different educational institutions are running their respective campus radio with different purposes and in different ways.

As a form of community radio, campus radio shares many of its basic characteristics with other forms, but it has some unique characteristics as well. It can be compared with other forms of community radio in the following ways–

- *Range of community*: As an essential condition, campus radio also serves a clearly specified community like other CRs that has to be geographically defined. But it serves the community of two types–student community inside the campus and immediate neighboring community around the campus. That is, students inside the campus of the educational institution running campus radio forms its essential community whereas students may or may not be a part of community radio run by NGOs, KVKs or other kind of institutions. For example, Radio Sharda in Jammu & Kashmir aims at serving the community of displaced Hindus whereas Radio Jamia states that its aim is to cater to its student community as well as general community living around the campus that comprises of industrial area and some villages near Okhla.
- *Operating the radio station:* Operating a community radio includes planning, conducting, recording of programs, inviting guests, keeping records and archives, writing scripts, making schedules, operating technical infrastructure like microphones, audio consoles and radio editing software. These tasks are done mainly by students in a campus radio whereas other CRs have professional personnel or volunteers from different walks of life who operate the station as part of their salaried job. Though community members also participate in the tasks of campus radio, but students of that campus form an essential component of the team. This can be seen, on one hand, as operating of the station at the level of amateurs instead of professionals, while on the other hand, this results in sensitizing the young students towards the

issues being faced by marginalized and undeveloped communities in the society along with development of leadership quality and training them to become professional RJ's, announcers, editors, presenters, scriptwriters in future.

A student recording in the for M.O.P. CR, M.O.P. Vaishnav College for Women, Tamil Nadu

Source: The Hindu

- *Setting up basic infrastructure:* The basic infrastructure required to set up campus radio is the same as that required in the other forms of CR. It includes microphones, recorder, audio console, computer system, transmitter, antenna, set of speakers, recording and editing software, one room to set up the system. Government of India runs different schemes under which this infrastructure can be bought and set up at different kinds of institutions with the assistance of proper agency. A minor difference in this context is that it is mandatory for the educational institutions to locate the antenna and transmitter of the radio station inside the campus boundary whereas in case of all others, these can be located anywhere in the geographical limits of the community the station is aiming to serve.

- *Application process and grant of license:* There is a similar initial process for all types of community radio by applying online for the license. After filling the online application form, every applicant can keep a track of its status through a Comprehensive Radio Management Information System. But the process varies a little bit within the category of educational institutions. The colleges, universities or schools set up by the government have to get an approval from a committee comprising of members from different ministries whereas the application of private educational institutions need an approval from Ministry of Defense, Human Resource and that of Home Affairs separately.
- *Managing human resource*: Managing human resource deals with managing the persons working for a community radio. In case of campus radio, the personnel managing and operating it consists of students, faculty members and people from neighboring community. Since the students of different batches and faculty in-charge remain associated with it permanently, the station hardly gets affected with a change in the members of community who co-ordinate, participate and present its programs. But in case of other forms of CR, especially the one run by an NGO, the station is more or less dependent on the people of that region/ community who either volunteer or work for the station as its reporters in the field or announcers in the studio or managing the guests and artists on the station. Since these tasks are comparatively low paid, they leave the station upon getting a permanent job elsewhere. This makes it hard for the organization to manage its human resource.
- *Representation of community members:* Like other categories of CRs, Campus radio too has to abide by the regulation of I&B Ministry which says that its 50% content, at least, should be generated with

participation of local community for which the station has been set up. Further, it is also mandatory that the management of the station should be reflective of the community, i.e. it should have representation of all the groups in the community. To serve this purpose, managing committee and program committee of the station comprises of community members in all kinds of institutions. For example, at Anna FM (Anna University), each faculty member plans program content of each day by consulting media student volunteers and neighboring community members. At Radio Mewat (SMART NGO), all of its 10 reporters are from community and the managing committee consists of a panchayat member, Urdu teacher, *Maulvi*, Head of NGO, NABARD Officer, Zilla Paarshad, Deputy Director of Agriculture Department

- *Broadcast of news and commercials:* Campus radio and other CRs follow the same instruction of I&B Ministry that no such program is allowed to be broadcast that relates to news and current affairs and is otherwise political in nature. In case of commercials as well, same rule applies on all forms of CRs that no sponsored programs are allowed except those sponsored by Central & State Government & other organizations to broadcast public information. The advertisements are limited to 5 minutes per program and that too of local events, business, announcements of local services and jobs.
- *Financial stability:* Since the basic cost of setting up and running of a full-fledged and well-equipped CR in campus is borne by the educational institution itself from its fund received or created for the same, the station gets the remaining fund by collaborating with outside agencies. But in case of other forms of CRs, the cost of setting up is borne by the organization itself and the for the remaining expenses, they are entirely dependent on the projects with bankers or

development agencies or *panchayats* etc. For example, Community Radio Gurgaon Ki Awaaz started its journey by using egg trays in studios for the purpose of sound proofing whereas in case of Radio Jamia, the station is funded from the Development Fund of the University.

- *Maintenance of infrastructure:* Maintenance of infrastructure refers to protecting it from rain, dust, temperature variations, humidity, heat etc. which can damage the equipments. Since the availability of rooms and set up of quality infrastructure is provided properly by the educational institution, maintaining and replacement of recorders, air conditioner or console is not difficult. But in other cases, especially the one run by NGO, it difficult to maintain infrastructure, more difficult because the station essentially operates within a rural, isolated, tribal areas with a low running budget.
- *Program code and advertising code:* All forms of CR have to follow the code prescribed for All India Radio by the government with regard to the kind of advertisements and program content broadcast on the airwaves.

Involvement of Community

Different campus radio stations devise various program formats as per the needs of community they serve. For planning these, an assessment of cultural, social and development needs of the community is done by students and analyzed for deciding the theme and writing the script of program. Case Study I demonstrates this participatory process in HCCCR (90.4 MHz) at Holy Cross College. Generally, the programs include cultural programs, talks, discussion by community members on issues affecting the community, phone-ins, interviews, drama etc. Case Study II shows how themes are chosen as per the needs of the community in DUCR (90.4 MHz) at Delhi University.

CASE STUDY-I

Voice of the Unheard

TIRUCHIRAPPALLI:, OCTOBER 24, 2016 13:15 IST

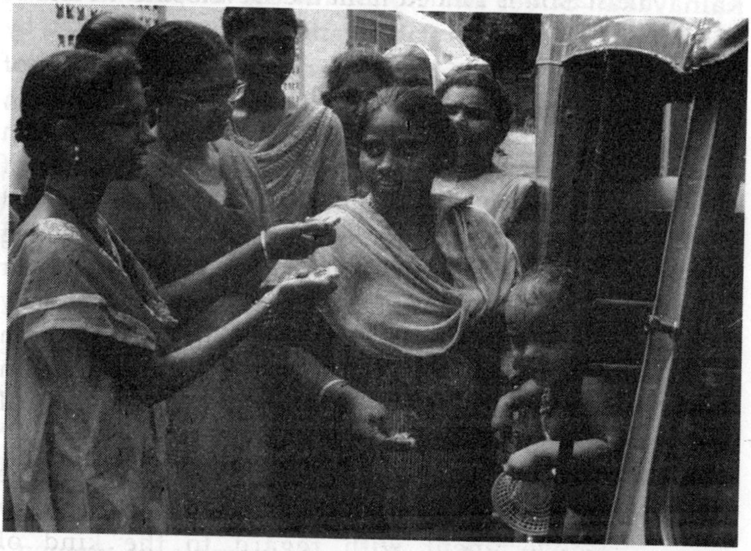

Holy Cross College's Community Radio service helps to bridge underprivileged families in the vicinity

Source: The Hindu

Ten years after it was inaugurated, Tiruchi's Holy Cross College Community Radio (HCCCR) 90.4 MHz continues to reach out to a small circle of listeners with programmes in Tamil that are a mix of public service messages and student journalism.

"Most of our students are from rural areas and first-generation learners. Once they are exposed to the radio, and get trained in broadcasting, they pick up lots of self-confidence. When they listen to their own voice on radio, they are just taken up," says Sister Bridget Chelladurai, who has been in charge of the radio at Holy Cross College for the past two years.

With a transmitter that caters to a radius of around 5 to 6 kilometers around the college, HCCCR's listeners are mostly based in the slums of Jeevanagar, Dharmanathapuram, Kalnayakan Street and Kolathamedu. Besides in-house orientation, the station's staff members have been trained by Commonwealth Educational Media Centre for Asia in New Delhi. The programmes are broadcast in two repeat shifts, from 6 a.m. to 10 a.m. and 4 p.m. to 8 p.m.

The main challenge in maintaining listener interest, says assistant station manager M. Geethalakshmi, is in creating content completely devoid of commercial and political themes.

"When we started out, most of the listeners would ask why we didn't have film songs. But we have tried to change their tastes to other programmes. We have managed to employ some 5 people from the community to work exclusively for the radio, who are paid separately for their services," she says.

Geethalakshmi herself is an example of women's empowerment triggered by the community radio service. A high school graduate, Geethalakshmi became interested in broadcasting and interned in HCCCR before she was appointed as its assistant training manager.

She is also pursuing higher education at Holy Cross College.

"I stay in Jeeva Nagar, which is very close to the college. So I walk to work everyday," says Geethalakshmi, who formally joined the service in 2008. "My husband works as a turner and has been very supportive since the beginning."

Travelling in an aeroplane for the very first time and addressing a national-level meeting on community radio are some of her proudest moments related to HCCCR. The radio's schedule includes programmes on health, sanitation, cookery, education, employment, market and gold rates.

For S. Arulraj, F.M. station manager, community radio production is more difficult than that of a commercial service because of the many restrictions on the material. "Everything has to be more sober and subtle," says Arulraj, who started out in animation before switching over to audio production. "As we cannot use sound clips from film songs, we have to create our own short musical interludes."

In 2008-09, HCCCR conducted 'Pudhiya Jananam' (New Birth), a Science for Women project commissioned by the Department of Science and Technology, New Delhi with a grant of Rs. 16 lakhs. The programmes were targeted at raising awareness among women of Jeeva Nagar and Dharmanathapuram on subjects like science, health and hygiene.

India had only 180 operational community radio stations as on May 1, 2015, according to a study published by Factly.com. They were mooted first in 2002, when they were restricted to educational institutions. Since 2006, non-governmental organizations and other grassroots bodies in agriculture and social services have been allowed to start community radio stations.

The projected growth of community radio has yet to take off because of excessive licensing and centralized government control, say analysts. Holy Cross College's community radio is said to be the only one of its kind in south Tamil Nadu, but few people are really aware of its presence. "It is only has a limited outreach right now, so we are not doing much. But we are trying to maximise its use among our students. If we give them outdoor microphones to add more interviews," says Sr. Bridget.

"The station is inside the campus, and if the students are regular for 30 programmes for 3 years, we give them a certificate. This is boosts their self-esteem. Sometimes they get their programmes re-recorded on CDs and take it home to listen with their parents," says Sr. Bridget. "It may be very low technology, but as it was proven in last year's floods in coastal Tamil Nadu, it was radio that contributed to the success of the relief efforts. Community radio gives a voice to the unheard."

CASE STUDY-II

Learn Your Legal Rights with Delhi University Community Radio

By Siddhanta Mishra | Published: 05th November 2016 11:39 PM

Source: New Indian Express

NEW DELHI: To sensitise the youth about their legal rights, the Delhi Legal Service Authority (DLSA) in association with the Delhi University Community Radio (DUCR) have invited 11 High Court judges for 11 episodes on 11 topics, including sexual harassment, victim compensation, arrest, domestic violence and consumer protection.

"The courts need to be made more accessible to provide real 'access to justice'. We have adorned the new role of working in dissemination of legal knowledge among people. DUCR, which is run by student volunteers, will enlighten marginalised masses with its radio programmes," said Chetna

Singh, a judge who spoke about sexual harassment at workplace.

The judges will talk about the issues and answer queries of radio jockeys. The first episode was broadcasted Saturday night at the DU north campus.

"The objective of the project is to make aware, the students and staff of each college about the basic legal literacy. People know that the courts provide transparent judgment but not many know how to approach court," said Mohit Gupta, project leader and third year LLB student at DU.

The varsity has also written to the Ministry of Broadcasting for phase two of the project, in which they will connect a loop with the community radio in the country. In the 30 to 40-minute session, student volunteers ask questions to the judges, said Gayathri Mani, a student volunteer. The radio show is available on 90.4 MHz within a radius of 10-12 km.

"It is important that the students get relevant legal information on time. DUCR and DSLSA have taken the right step in this direction by launching a series of radio programmes on legal issues," said Monika Saroha, another judge, who spoke on senior citizens' rights.

Managed by a team of 400 students, the DUCR was established by former Union Minister Kapil Sibal in 2007.

New Trends in Campus Radio

Many of the campus radio stations in India are adopting different techniques of reaching more and more audiences in the globalized era. This involves different applications of new media - websites, streaming media and smart phones. This has added a new dimension to the communicating power of this medium as campuses are uploading their programs on their exclusive websites after broadcasting them on air. Adoption of 'net-only 'radio by Indian Institute of Technology Kanpur (IIT K) and the launch of *'Vidyavani'* campus radio on web by University of Pune demonstrates the new ways of distributing campus radio content. According to Andrea Barker (2010), *"net-only radio differs markedly from traditional radio and radio online as it is a low cost venture, does not need offices or institutional arrangements and is more flexible in terms of format and non-format broadcasting."* Introduction of DUCR mobile app by Delhi University campus radio is the next step that provides reach to global student community while managing and producing content for the local one.

Another trend is the launch of *'Campus Radio Initiative'* by private companies like Britannia MEC, Radio Mirchi, Gaana .com. With their stated objective of 'uniting the voice of youth', these are creating a new platform out of the college campuses through mobile phones. While this kind of involvement of young students looks certainly a positive step, there is a need to be careful about any possible hidden agenda or purpose behind such interactions and discussions with the young minds. It is important to maintain the not-for-profit, democratic and participatory nature of this medium to make it serve, in real sense, the communities it is meant for.

List of Campus Radio Stations Operating in India (2016)*

S.No.	*Campus Radio*	*Name of Educational Institution*
1	SUFM CRS	Sri Venketeswara Oriental College, Tirupati, AP
2	Radio Vishnu	Sri Vishnu Engg. College form Women, Bhimavarm, AP
3	GMR Radio	GMR Institute of Technology, Srikakulam, AP
4	ANU Radio	Acharya Nagarjuna University Guntur, AP
5	Jnan Taranga	Krishna Kanta Handique State Open University, Assam
6	Uttam Radio	Indian Instituite of Business Managemenmt, Patna, Bihar
7	Vivek CR	Vivek High School, Chandigarh
8	Jyotirgamaya CR	Punjab University, Chandigarh
9	Radio Raman	Dr. CV Raman University, Bilaspur, Chattisgarh
10	Neotech CR	Neotech Technical and Management School, Chattisgarh
11	Apna Radio	Indian Institute of Mass Communication, Delhi
12	DU CR	University of Delhi, Delhi

(Contd...)

13	Jamia Radio	AJK MCRC Jamia Millia Islamia, Delhi
14	JIMS CR	Jkagannath Institute of Management Studies, Rohini, Delhi
15	Radio JIMS	Jagannath International Management School, Vasant Kunju, Delhi
16	Vallabh Vidyanagar Campus Radio	Sardar Patel University, Vallabh Vidyanagar, Gujarat
17	Micavaani	Mudra Institute of Communications Ahmedabad, Gujarat
18	Guruvaani Radio	Educational Multimedia Research Centre, Gujarat University, Gujarat
19	Radio Sirsa	Chaudhary Devilal University, Haryana
20	JG Radio	Bharat Sainik Sr. Sec. School, Haryana
21	Radio NGF	NGF College of Engineering & Technology, Haryana
22	Hamara MSPICM	MS Pawar Institute of Communication and Management, Solan, HP
23	Tashi Delek CR	Tibetan Children's Village School, HP
24	Ramana Dhwani	Shree Ramanna Academy for Blind, Banglore, Karnataka
25	Rdaio ACtive	Sri Bhagwan Mahavir Jain College, Banglore, Karnataka
26	Radio Siddhartha	Sri Siddhartha Centre for Media Studies, Tumkur, Karnataka
27	Radio Manipal	Manipal academy of Higher Education, Manipal, Karnataka
28	Antarvani CRS	Shambaveshwar Vidya Vardhak Sangh, Karnataka
29	Radiop Sarang	St. Aloysius College, Karnataka
30	Radio Universal	Universal College , Vijaynagar, Banglore, Karnataka
31	Janadhwani	Vivek School of Excellence, Karnataka
32	KLE Dhwani	B.V. Bhoomaraddi College of Engineering & Technology, Karnataka
33	Venudhwani CR	K L E Academy of Higher Education and Research, Karnataka
34	Ninada CR	Shri Dharamsthala Manjuunatheshwara College, Karnataka
53	Radio MACFAST	Mar Athanasios College of Advanced Studies, Kerala
36	Radio DC	DC School of Management and Technology, Kottayam, Kerala
37	Radio Media Village	St. Joseph College of Communication, Kerala
38		Global Educational Net, Kerala

(Contd...)

39	Radio Popcorn	RKDF institute of Science & Technology, Bopal , Madhya Pradesh
40	Vanya Radio Sesaipura	Govt. High School, Sesaipura, MP
41	Vanya Radio Nalchha	Shaskiya Utkrishta Ucchtar Madhyamik Vidyalay, Nalccha, Dhar, MP
42	Radio Chandra Shekkhar Azaad Nagar	Shaskiya Utkrishta Ucchtar Madhyamik Vidyalay, Bhabra, MP
43	Vanya Radio Khalwa	Shaskiya Utkrishta Ucchtar Madhyamik Vidyalay, Khalwa, MP
44	Vanya Radio Chicholi	Shaskiya Utkrishta Ucchtar Madhyamik Vidyalay, Distt. Betul, MP
45	Vidyavani CR	University of Pune, Maharashtra
46	Radio FTII	Film and Television Institute of India, Pune, Maharashtra
47	Dnyanvani	Padmshree Dr. D.Y.Patil Vidyapeeth, Navi Mumbai, Maharashtra
48	Vasundhara Krushivahini	Vidya Pratisthan's Institute of Information Technology, Baramati, Pune, Maharashtra
49	MUST Radio	University of Mumbai, Mumbai, Maharashtra
50	Radio Mast	Mahatma Gandhi Vidyamandir's M.S.G. Art, Science & Commerce College, Maharashtra
51	Voice of SOA Community	Siksha O Anusandhaan University, Orissa
52	Ravenshaw Radio	Ravenshaw University, Orissa
53	NILA FM	Sri Manakula Vinayagar Engineering College, Pondicherry
54	Hony FM	Acharya Arts & Science College, Villanur, Pondicherry
55	Puduwai Vaani CRS	Pondicherry University, Pondicherry
56	GNGC CR	Guru Nanak Girls College, Ludhiana, Punjab
57	Radio Chitkara	Chitkara Educational Trust, Punjab
58	GNE 90.8 FM	Guru Nanak Dev Engineering College, Punjab
59	Radio 7	Inmdia International Institute of Management, Jaipur, Rajasthan
60	Radio Banasthali	Banasthali Vidyapeeth, Banasthali, Rajsathan
61	Radio Eminent	Eminent T.T. Girls College, Diggi. Malpura, Tonk, Rajasthan
62	Radio Madhuban	Prajapita Brahm Kumaris Ishwariya Vishwavidyalay a, Rajasthan

(Contd...)

63	Jyoti Vani CR	Jyoti vidyapeeth Women's University, Rajasthan
64	Kongu CRS	Kongu engineering College, Perundurai, Tamil Nadu
65	MOPCR	M.O.P. Vaishnav College for Women, chennai, Tamil Nadu
66	Mugil FM	Erode Sengunthar Engineering College, Erode, Tamil Nadu
67	Loyola CVR	Loyola College , Chennai, Tamil Nadu
68	Shyamalavani CR	Subhalakshmi College of science, Madurai, Tamil Nadu
69	Pasumai FM	Peace Industrial School, Dindigul, Tamil Nadu
70	HCCCR	Holy Cross college, Tiruchirapalli, Tamil Nadu
71	SRM Muthucharan CR	SRM College of Engineering, Distt. Kanchipuram, Tamil Nadu
72	PSG CR	PSG College of Technology, Peelamedu, Coimbatore,Tamil Nadu
73	Sivanthi CR	Aditanar College of Arts & Science, Tiruchendur, Tamil Nadu
74	PGP CR	PGP Educational and Welfare Society, Tamil Nadu
75	KSR CR	K.S.Rangasamy Educational Institutions, Tamil Nadu
76	MKC CR	M. Kumarasaamy College of Enguineering, Tamil Nadu
77	Anna CR	EMMRC, Anna University, Chennai
78	Kalpakkam CRS	Atomic Energy Central School No.2, Tamil Nadu
79	Ilanthalir CR	Rajiv Gandhi National Institute of Youth Development, Tamil Nadu
80	Rathinavani CR	Rathinam College of Arts & Science, Tamil Nadu
81	AGN School CRS	AGN School, Tamil Nadu
82	SSM CR	SSM College of Engineering, Tamil Nadu
83	VIT CR	VIT University, Tamil Nadu
84	Periyar CR	Periyar Mjaniamai College of Technology for Women, Thanjavur, Tamil Nadu
85	Bannari Amman CR	Bannari Amman Institute of Technology, Tamil Nadu
86	Pragnya CR	Gokaraju Rangaraju Institute of Engineering and Technology, Hyderabad, Telangana
87	KMIT Tarang	Keshav Memorial Education Society, Hyderabad, Telangana
88	Bol Hyderabad	Hyderabad University, Hyderabad
89	Ghazipur CR	PG College, Ghazipur, UP
90	CMS Radio	City Montessori School, Lucknow, UP

(Contd...)

91	CMS DC CR	CMS Degree college, Lucknow, UP
92	Radio IIMT	IIMT College, Meerut, UP
93	Salaam Namaste	Institute of Management Studies, UP
94	IITK CR	IndiAN Institute of Technology, Kanpur, UP
95	Radio Noida	Asian School of Media Studies, UP
96	HINT CR	HINT Inmstitute of Mass Communication, UP
97	Agra ki Awaaz	Dr. B.R.A. University, UP
98	Radio Amity	Amity University, UP
99	BBD CR	Babu Banarsidas University, UP
100	Suno Sharda	Sharda University , UP
101	Radio SD	SD College of Pharmacy & Vocational Studies, UP
102	NIOS CR	National Institute of Open Schooling, UP
103	NIVH Hello Doon	National Institute of the Visually Handicapped, Uttarakhand
104	Pantnagar Janvani	GB Pant University of Agriculture and Technology, Uttarakhand
105	Himgiri Ki Awaaz	Himgiri Nabh Vishwavidyalay, Uttarakhand
106	Hello Haldwani	Uttarakhand Open University, Uttarakhand
107	Radio Khushi	Guru Nanak Fifth Centenary School, Mussorie, Uttaranchal
108	Radio JU	Jadavpur University, West Bengal
109	NSHM CR	NSHM Institute of Media and Communication, West Bengal
110	Radio Adan	School of Film and Mass Communication, Institute of Agriculture Technology and Sciences

5

Search for Campus Radio in Community Radio Policy Formulations

Dr. Susmita Bala

In 21st century the whole concept of mass communication has been challenged. It is believed that there could be no such communication which can cater to the masses, and which can be within the reach of masses. Mass is difficult to define; and reaching out the masses with a single communication through a single media platform seem impossible.

So, scholars agree that communication has to be targeted and for this purpose we need to do the segmentation of audience. With any available communication technology, the message has to be sent to the targeted group. The content and structuring of the message has to be as per the information needs and comprehension level of the targeted group.

Conceptualizing Campus Radio in Community Broadcasting

The conceptual changes in mass communication have taken us to the concept of community communication, which can

Dr. Susmita Bala is Professor and Head, Journalism and Mass Communication, Delhi Metropolitan Education (DME), Guru Gobind Singh Indraprastha University, Delhi. She has been teaching in BhartiyaVidya Bhavan and India Today Media Institute (ITMI) for long.

be done by using different media platforms. Radio can be one such platform. This has led to the emergence of community broadcasting, which is a departure from conventional broadcasting.

Departure from Conventional Broadcasting

In conventional broadcasting broadcasters and listeners are two distinct sets of people. The broadcasters are involved in information collection, structuring and dissemination, while listeners are merely receivers. Though efforts have been made to bridge the gap between broadcasters and listeners by introducing phone-in programmes and other methods of participatory communication, yet the distance is significant in conventional broadcasting.

Community broadcasting is a complete departure in the sense that there is just one party, one set of people involved in broadcasting and listening. Both, the broadcasters and the listeners are involved in generation of content and using the content for their own benefit. In community radio, broadcasting turns into narrowcasting which increases the credibility of communication.

Defining Community Broadcasting

As defined by Commonwealth Educational Media Centre for Asia (CEMCA), community broadcasting is considered the third model of radio broadcasting since it adds to commercial broadcasting and public service broadcasting. Community stations serve geographic communities and communities of interest. The community radio stations broadcast content that is popular and relevant to a local, specific audience.

Community radio stations are operated, owned, and influenced by the communities served by them. These are generally non-profit and provide a mechanism for enabling individuals, groups, and communities to tell their own stories, to share experiences and, in a media-rich world, to become creators and contributors of media.

Defining Campus Radio Broadcasting

Mostly, campus radio stations have been set up for the purpose of broadcasting educational programmes, though some campus radio stations are operated for the purpose of training professional radio personnel. In some countries campus radio stations promote non-commercial music. They often provide promotional exposure to new and emerging local artists.

Thus, campus radio, also known as college radio, university radio or student radio, is a type of radio station that is run by the students of a college, university or any other educational institution. Programming may be exclusively by the students, or may include the members of the listening community in the broadcast area of the radio station.

Implications of the Study of Community/Campus Radio

In 1995, Supreme Court of India came out with a landmark judgment, stating that airwaves or frequencies are public property and cannot be controlled by the government. This prepared ground for the decontrolling of the radio and the television sector, which eventually led to the opening of both the sectors to non-government players.

In 1996, Paswan Committee pushed for non-commercial broadcasting and recommended that the university and other educational institutions should be allowed to setup radio stations so as to ensure dissemination of information at the grass root level within the community. In view of the Supreme Court judgment and the recommendations of Paswan Committee, the government opened the radio broadcasting to private companies in the year 2000 and to universities/ educational institutions in 2002.

Though the policy launched in 2002 was named as community radio policy, it was only for educational institutions. Even after revision in policy in 2006, the focus remained on radio stations setup by educational institutions. In spite of the fact that the government did not name the policy as campus radio policy like in many other parts of the world;

the majority of community radio stations opened up after 2006 were set up inside campuses of educational institutions.

Studying Community/Campus Radio in India

Since campus radio stations have gradually acquired significant status in the current broadcasting scenario of the country, there is a pertinent need to find out what is so distinct about these radio stations. How do these radio stations function and benefit the community? So, this study remains confined to understanding community broadcasting and functioning of operational community radio stations of universities and other educational institutions.

The study is focused to find out the thrust of community broadcasting in India and whether the government has taken due care of radio stations set up by universities and other educational institutions on their campus while formulating policy in this regard. Also, what is the status and functioning of such campus radio stations and what benefits are reaching the communities by their programming.

This study comprises looking into the community radio policy documents and analyzing the outcome of implementation on the policy, with special emphasis on radio stations set up by universities and other educational institutions on their campus. This includes study of the management, administration and functioning of such campus radio stations, involving analyses of the issues of content, production and broadcast of programmes.

Definition of Campus Radio Station

Though there is one single policy for community radio which also comprises radio stations set up by educational institutions, there are separate set of rules for community radio stations set up by NGOs and the stations set up by educational institutions. Since the distinct identity of campus radio stations has not been acknowledged in the policy, there is an imperative need to decide an operational definition of campus radio.

Based on practices in other countries, the following definition of campus radio seems most appropriate for this study.

Campus Radio is a radio station, setup by any educational institution like university or college, after obtaining license from the government as per approved community radio policy. The university or college must be an institution established by the central/state government or by a private entity as per law.

Importing Campus Radio to Community Radio Policy Formulations

Broadcasting in India got an impetus in the last decade of the 20th century. Supreme Court judgment (1996) stated that airwaves are public property; and Paswan Committee (1996) recommended that non-commercial broadcasting stations should be setup and run by universities and other educational institutions. During this period, a community broadcasting movement had already started on the ground.

Approach of the Government towards Community Broadcasting

So, the government made up its mind of formalizing the community broadcasting in the country by bringing a policy. Since the policy launch in 2002, the approach of the government has been to boost community radio movement for giving impetus to community development at the grass root level. The government has assigned for itself the role of a facilitator, expecting that the civil society and educational bodies would take the lead. The government, in fact, wants to make sure that this movement is built by augmenting capacity building in the society.

However, this has proved an idealistic approach. By confining it to the formulation of the policy and providing a legal framework for community radio stations would not apparently suffice in Indian society where social and voluntary organizations are not so equipped. Experts feel that the government has to be pro-active to make community broadcasting a success. With policy support financial support is also required for the erection and sustenance of community radio broadcasting infrastructure.

Major Policy Developments Regarding Community Radio

Community radio policy 2002was campus radio policy for all practical purposes since it allowed the universities and other educational institutions to set up their own radio stations. However, the desired result did not come as apathy permeated the educational institutions. There appeared to be lack of clarity with regard to the objective of community radio broadcasting. So, the government decided to broad base the policy by opening it outside educational institutions.

In 2006, this policy was revised and expanded, and NGOs were also allowed to setup community radio stations. The revised policy entitled community radio stations to collect advertisements from the local area and broadcast these advertisements for five minutes in an hours' time. This enraged the private FM operators as they thought that the collection of local advertisements, which might be commercial in nature, would be an infringement in their domain. But, the government stood on with TRAI recommendations at its back.

While setting up and sustaining a community radio station remained an issue, the government announced a policy addition in 2009 and extended the benefit of government advertisements to community radio stations. Earlier, print media organizations, TV channels and private FM radio channels used to get government advertisements.

In 2012, the government launched a scheme named as Community Radio Support Scheme(CRSS) for providing financial assistance in the procurement of equipment. CRSS was brought to help the organizations which were financially not strong in setting up community radio station. This scheme reduced the initial cost since the government agreed to meet the fifty per cent cost of the equipment at the stage of their installation. The government also announced Emergency Grant and the Innovation Grant to community radio stations.

All the schemes mentioned above are available to all kinds of community radio stations including those which have been setup by educational institutions. So, campus radio stations have not been exclusively benefitted in any way through these schemes.

Policy Interventions in the Process of Policy-making

It is worth mentioning here that many NGOs and voluntary organizations have been working in the field of community broadcasting. Prominent among them are CRF, CRA, Maara, CEMCA and Ford Foundation. These organizations have been working in close cooperation with the government and have been extending all kind of help in making the community broadcasting a success.

The major activities of these organizations include conducting workshops for updating the skills of community radio professionals and awareness workshops for those who wish to setup community radio under some institution. Seminars, symposiums and conferences are also organized on a regular basis. These organizations also undertake field studies, which is more an academic exercise, but which could provide substantial base for any policy revision by the government. One significant job has been done in this regard by CRF by issuing a working paper.

It may be mentioned that policy additions of 2009 and 2012 were taken up by the government following academic input provided by these organizations. The persuasion from these organizations has motivated the government to act. The government is even refrained by these organizations if it indulges in any regressive step which might be detrimental to the growth of community radio. For instance in 2012, the government hiked the spectrum fee from Rs 19,700 to Rs 91,000 which was opposed by CRF, CRA and other organizations. Finally, the government had to roll back.

Success of the Policy in Terms of Spread of Radio Stations

Over the years community/campus radio stations have spread all across the country. As per latest figures released by the Ministry of Information and Broadcasting on November 1, 2016, India has 200 Operational community radio stations. [Source: website of Ministry of Information and Broadcasting]

The status of the last two years follows.

- Operational community radio stations (July 1, 2014) = 170
- Operational community radio stations (June 10, 2015) = 184
- Operational community radio stations (November 1, 2016) = 200
- These figures are self-explanatory. In almost two-and-a-half years (2014-2016), only 30 community radio stations have become operational.

As per policy guidelines, issued by the Ministry of Information and Broadcasting, an applicant should get community radio license within 10 months. But, figures of the last 12 years (2004-2016) establish that an applicant organization succeeds in clearing all the hurdles and getting a license in 2 to 3 years.

It may be noted here that the policy of community radio was announced in 2002, but the first radio station could come up only in 2004. Post revision of community radio policy in 2006, the first radio station could come up only in 2008.

To look into the progress chart since 2006 revised policy, 38 radio stations became operational in two years, 68 radio stations came in operation in four years. Further, the number of operational radio increased to 126 in six years, 170 in eight years and 200 in 10 years. This proves the point that the licensing process continues to be cumbersome despite efforts made by the government to make the process flexible.

Looking into the figures of campus radio stations, it should be noted that 63% community radio stations belong to universities and other educational institutions. In this study, such radio stations are being treated as campus radio stations. So, clubbing these radio stations with the ones setup by NGOs appears confusing.

Suggestions for Making Community/campus Radio Policy Effective

Community radio policy requires multiple changes so as to make it effective. These changes can be discussed likewise.

- A CR cell should be constituted in the Ministry of Communication should be set up following the pattern of the Ministry of Information and Broadcasting.
- SACFA clearance procedure should be simplified.
- Enhanced financial support should be provided to the organizations setting up community radio to meet the initial cost.
- A separate category of campus radio station should be acknowledged and separate set of guidelines should be framed for that.
- Communities in respect of campus radio stations should be properly defined. Catering to both on campus and off campus listeners appears confusing, particularly keeping in view their diverse information needs.

Campus Radio Station: Setup, Infrastructure and Funding

Campus radio stations are mostly headed by professional persons. These are either working or retired (from AIR) radio professionals, and their services are hired by the concerned campus radio station.

Management/Administration of Campus Radio Stations

As per community radio policy, the management has to be inclusive and accountable to the larger community. But, that inclusion is missing in campus radio stations. The management and the administrative setup in campus radio stations do not include any representative from the community. The only exception, to some extent, is DUCR which has set up a Programme Committee and Programme Sub-Committee comprising teachers, and Students' Core Group Student Coordinators to give representation to students in administrative structure.

Infrastructural Facilities for Production and Broadcasting

All essential infrastructural facilities are mostly available in campus radio stations. Every radio station has at least one studio for all production and broadcast purposes. There is nothing significant in transmission facilities. Following the provisions of community radio policy guidelines, every campus radio station has installed an FM transmitter of 50 Watt and an antenna of 30 meters of height.

It may be noted that campus radio stations which are linked to media departments of their parent institute are better placed in terms of infrastructure, production and broadcasting facilities. DU does not have a media department of its campus, and so it is in a disadvantageous position. DUCR still functions from a makeshift infrastructure.

Funding and Related Issues

There are three important issues which must be understood clearly. *One*, funding, *two*, revenue generation, *three*, sustainability

Funding: The government did not have any provision for funding since the inception of community radio policy, apparently for one simple reason that it wanted the community radio movement to grow in the society with government not seen a player. When it did not work, the government decided to come out with Community Radio Support Scheme(CRSS) in 2012. As per this scheme, the government helps the license holders in acquiring equipment by meeting their 50 per cent cost up to 7.5 lakhs. The government even announced Emergency Grant and Innovation Grant.

There are no figures available to find out how much money the government has spent under this scheme in recent years and how much benefits have reached the community radio stations.

Advertising: As per community radio policy guidelines (2006), community radio stations are allowed to broadcast 5 minutes of local advertisements in an hour's time. They are also entitled to get government advertisements as per policy announcement in 2009.

No figures are available as to how many community radio organizations have got themselves empanelled with DAVP for getting government advertisements. Also, no figures are available as to how much money community radio organizations have received during recent years as part of the government advertisement scheme. So, the success of the local advertisement policy and the government advertising policy cannot be ascertained.

However, experts from policy intervention groups feel that getting government advertisements is a cumbersome process and so, the real benefits have not reached the community radio stations. The spot rates of government advertisements are also low, and community radio stations have been asking for a revision in the rates.

Sustenance: The government has been brining all kind of policies, as discussed above, for making the community radio stations sustainable. But, slow progress on the policy amply proves the point that these schemes somehow have not addressed the financial woos of community radio stations.

All the schemes mentioned above are available to all kinds of community radio stations including those which have been setup by educational institutions. But, campus radio stations are not really benefitted by these schemes. If at all benefits are reaching, that might be reaching the community radio stations setup by NGOs.

Campus Radio Programmes: Content, Formats and Designing

Content of Radio Programmes

Campus radio stations give priority to programmes on health, environment and social issues. Keeping in view the requirement of their main target listeners i.e. students, these radio stations give emphasis on education, career, counseling and entrepreneurship.

Also, in consideration of off campus community in neighbourhood areas, issues like women health, women rights, children and their rights and matters related to vulnerable sections of society are chosen for programmes.

Composition of Radio Programmes

Radio station programmes are always composed of spoken words and music. The only thing programmers need to decide is,in what proportion the two components should be mixed. However, spoken words dominate the programming of campus radio stations under study.

Formats of Radio Programmes

Three most common formats used by all the campus radio stations are discussion, talk and interview. This is followed by phone-in programmes. It may be noted that all these programmes are spoken word programmes.

In all the campus radio stations, music based programmes are produced and broadcast with lot of variety.

Designing of Radio Programmes

In campus radio stations, the programmes are designed essentially by the head of the radio station. In the case of universities and colleges which have a media department, the designing of programmes is controlled by the faculty members and students of these departments.

Two major questions arise here.

- What is the contribution of community in programme designing? Apparently, students play an active role in programme designing. But, this activity is seen mostly in DUCR, whereas in other radio stations the role of the students in programme designing is comparatively less sigficant.
- Then, what is the role of off campus community in programme designing? This appears very less except Radio Jamia where members of the neighbourhood community contribute as active participants.

Looking for the aspect of innovation in programming, we find that two types of innovative programmes are produced and broadcast by the concerned campus radio station. These are content oriented and listener specific programmes.

In-house Production of Programmes

As per community radio policy, 50 per cent content should be generated by a radio station with the participation of local community. However, we find that campus radio stations produce 80 to 90 per cent programmes in-house by making use of their own resources. Thus, they are way ahead of the policy requirement.

Still, the question of the involvement and participation of local community requires further probe. Another related question is how to identify local community for a campus radio station?

It is found that the students and teachers inside the campus and cross-section of people outside the campus, they all contribute towards production of programmes. Besides this, the production people employed in a campus radio station also produce programmes.

Outsourcing of Programmes

Community radio policy permits the outsourcing of programmes.Campus radio stations acquire programmes from outside agencies with a view to infuse something new and innovative in the programmes.

The programmes are procured mainly from three types of organisations; AIR and central government ministries and departments, NGOs working in social sector and international agencies including embassies and high commissions.

Campus Radio Communities: Classification and Participation

Identification of Communities

There has always been confusion on the issue of identification of communities of campus radio station. This confusion originates from the community radio policy only. While community radio stations setup by NGOs have one community, radio stations setup by universities and educational institutions have two communities, one is the immediate community i.e. on campus community, and another is adopted but nebulous community off the campus.

The community members on the campus may not be interested in the programmes of campus radio station, since they are exposed to other media outlets and have the option of choosing the content of their interest elsewhere. The community outside the campus may not be interested in the programmes of campus radio station, since they would have little participation in the programmes and have no interest in expert driven content.

So, which community a campus radio station is supposed to address. The answer is both, keeping in view the existing policy. The existing campus radio stations cater to both the communities, on the campus and off the campus.

Exposure of Communities

The communities have limited exposure to campus radio station. They always look at either private FM radio stations or AIR FM channels. It has been found that campus radio stations face a tough time in urban areas because exposure of communities, both on the campus and off the campus, has no bounds.

Those who listen to campus radio stations do not do it on a daily basis. They might be tuning in a campus radio station either once in two days or once in three days, or even more. Some community members listen to a campus radio station as and when required. This happens in the case of students or potential students as they try to get update information regarding admission on the concerned campus radio station.

Involvement and Participation of Communities

In spite of discouraging signs, the involvement of community members in the broadcast of community radio station is confirmed by the fact that those who listen to the programmes do it with apt attention. Such listeners mostly retain in mind whatever they would have listened during the broadcast. The listeners are even in the habit of making use of the input that they would have received during a broadcast.

The community members even participate in the programmes of campus radio station. They do it as script writer, anchor, interviewer and singer. However, it is felt that lot more is to be done to woo the community members to get associated with campus radio stations. Some awareness campaigns need to be launched. Some tangible or intangible benefits need to be offered.

Benefits and Beneficiaries

It is difficult to assess what are the benefits attached with campus radio broadcast. It is believed that community members listen to the programmes of campus radio stations since these are refreshing and entertaining. They are also benefitted in terms of addition to their knowledge.

On the campus, students are benefitted the most by the programmes of campus radio stations. Off the campus, the beneficiaries do not belong to a particular section or profession.

But, one important section draws attention i.e. housewives and elderly people in the neighbourhood of campus radio stations.

Policy Paradoxes and Resolution

Characteristics of Community Radio/campus Radio

The characteristics of community radio and campus radio are different. The policy makers have simply added confusion by making a common policy for both. Community radio stations are setup by the community for its own sake, and the same set of people are involved in content generation and content receiving. An NGO setting up a community radio station is considered to have emerged from within the community where it is functioning.

Campus radio stations are setup by universities and other educational institutions on their campuses for the benefit of community. The policy makers expect that these community radio stations identify, define and adopt a community which is close to the campus and falls within the 10 kms radius of the radio station. But, the educational institution cannot leave its primary community i.e. students.

Functioning of Community/Campus Radio Stations

The management structure of a community radio station should be inclusive, and accountable to the community. This is what has been stated in the community radio policy of the government.

It is learnt that in community radio stations setup by NGOs, members of the community function as Management. They themselves decide what kind of content should be chosen for programmes, and then they themselves make the programmes which they themselves would listen along with fellow community members.

No such thing happens in the case of campus radio stations. Here, the programmes are produced by hired professionals, for listeners who are placed either on the campus of the educational institution or outside the campus.

Campus radio stations, unlike community radio stations, belong to a privileged community. The community of campus radio stations is privileged to have access to education, access to technology and access to financial resources.

The information needs of the community of campus radio stations are different. The government should not force its development mandate on these radio stations. If campus radio stations are broadcasting for the students, development programming (going by the definition stated by the government in policy guidelines and elsewhere) appear redundant.

Campus radio stations should have freedom to choose their content which is fresh, original, interesting and also catchy, so as to grab more ears. No purpose is served by producing uninteresting programmes for socially, economically and educationally developed class.

Participation and Involvement of Communities in Community/Campus Radio

Existing community radio policy insists on the involvement and participation of communities in the affairs of the radio station. The involvement is expected to encompass designing and production of programmes, and handling the broadcasting and transmission of programmes. In campus radio stations, all such jobs are performed by professional persons with the help of students. Outside community is hardly involved in any such task.

The job of scripting and anchoring is also handled either by hired professionals or by students, and outside community members are involved to a limited extent. There may be some exceptions to this; like in the case of Radio Jamia, members of the outside community handle scripting, anchoring and production.

In such circumstances, members of the outside community have turned into receivers i.e. listeners of campus radio stations. They are found mostly detached. Thus, there appears to be two sets of people, one producing the programmes and another consuming the programmes. This is apparently against the very concept of community broadcasting. So, there is a genuine need of taking out campus radio from the clutches of community radio.

Obligation on Policy-makers

So, the policymakers are required to frame separate policies for community radio and campus radio stations with clear set of guidelines that identify their respective mandate, communities and programming. Some structural changes must be introduced in respective policies, cosmetic changes in the existing policy can bear no fruits.

6

Community Radio: Policy and Challenges to Sustainability

Suruchi Shirish

Introduction

It is interesting to know that where other countries of South Asia has utilized the benefits of community radio, India has remained hesitant to explore this alternative media which could have helped in fostering the social change. The government was not open to the idea of sharing air waves or allowing non-governmental bodies, organizations or self help groups to use this basic technology to meet their information needs. For a country like India which have a very pluralistic society and consist of communities who have very different information needs, community radio can be an answer to such needs and demands. It is frequently stated that community radio is the most relevant form of media for socially excluded groups, due to its lower technological cost (both of the stations and receiver sets), low literacy levels required, and therefore, relatively low barriers to entry and participation (as cited by Bailur, 2012). One cannot deny the fact that community radio is not only affordable but it requires very basic or low literacy

Suruchi Shirish is presently teaching as Assistant Professor at Lady Shri Ram College, Department of Journalism, University of Delhi, Delhi.

levels to run a station, which is making it the most preferred community media, these reasons has made community radio quite popular not in developing countries but also in developed countries.

Communicative rights, including access to information and freedom of expression, are at the heart of democratic societies. An essential component of these rights is the ability to create one's own media independent of government or commercial pressure (Coyer & Hintz, 2013). The right to communicate and to have affordable access to the means of communication is increasingly being acknowledged throughout the world as a fundamental human rights. The Seventh World Congress of AMARC held in Milan, Italy, in 1998 emphasized on the first and equitable access to and participation in communication media for strengthening the rights of indigenous peoples, minorities, migrants and refugee. There was also focus on education and training to enable people to develop their own media and communication skills (Pavarala & Malik, 2007).

This third sector of media or also known as alternative media started emerging in most part of the world because the public broadcaster and commercial media failed to realize the actual information needs of people and, Pavarala & Malik (2007), states the diminishing plurality of information have eroded the diversity and quality of information in the public sphere, rendering civil society increasingly ineffective. Public service media are often too closely controlled by political interest, and commercial media carry burden of profit, leading scholars such as Hollander and Strappers (1992) to suggest that dominant media have compromised their legitimacy as genuine components of a true public sphere, where as community broadcaster are free from such constraints (cited by Loeser, 2016).

CR (community radio) became a popular medium against the public and commercial media in 1970s. Radio is an affordable medium when it comes to production, management as well as the reception part. Community radio is a non-profit service and does not aim at generating revenue as done by public or commercial media. Journey of community radio in India has not been an easy one, it took nearly a decade for the Government of India to draft a policy for it. In 1995 Supreme Court of India made a historic ruling and declared the airwaves as public property. But Indian government was not ready to allow a third sector to come up and allowed private broadcasters to use airwaves purely for entertainment purpose.

For Saeed (n.d.) radio broadcasting and within that community radio is by far the cheapest mode of disseminating information and education among communities that often live in hard to reach areas. Despite this or perhaps because of being a poor man's medium radio has got little or no place in the broadcasting policy framework of this country. The struggle for community radio has been a long one in India, where the government had its own inhibitions and on the other side the social activists favoured freedom of speech and expression and want to have a public sphere in true sense free of dominant, market oriented media. Government of India in 2002 opened FM radio to community groups and to university campuses. In 2006 the Union Cabinet formulated a new policy on community radio and today there are 191 operational Community Radio in India (Riaz & Qureshi, 2017)

Community Radio Policy Movement in India

Community Radio movement in India started soon after the Supreme Court of India came out with the landmark judgment in 1995 by declaring airwaves as public property and must be utilized for public good. As a result of this judgment, several media professionals, policy actors and civil society organizations gathered in Banglore in September 1996 to discuss the scope for community radio in India. They signed the Banglore Declaration, which subsequently became the basis of advocacy for community radio policy. Beyond India Community Radio Broadcasting was recognized as an essential public service in the Milan Declaration on Communication and Human Rights in August 1998 (Riaz & Qureshi, 2017).

In May 2000, Government of India interpreted the 1995 Supreme Court declaration and decided to allow commercial auctioning of airwaves to private media as a change from government monopoly. But there was no mention of community radio, the private players were allowed FM stations purely for entertainment. Again there was advocacy for community radio and argued for an interpretation of the judgment that would allow "a three tier" broadcasting structure for radio; this later became known as Pastapur Initiatives (Riaz & Qureshi, 2017). The Pastapur Declaration was a stepping stone as it urged government to create a three tier structure of broadcasting in India: non-profit community radio in addition to state owned public radio and private commercial radio (TRAI consultation paper, 2004). The UNESCO Pastapur Initiative on Community Radio sponsored workshop in 2000, was an effort to urge government to make media space available not only for private players but also to communities.

The country was going through the phase where government was taking decisions on liberalisation, privatisation and globalisation, but was not willing to liberate radio for community purpose and was reluctant to differentiate between commercial radio and community radio. "Avoiding recognition of the "non profit" and community-oriented nature of community radio would ensure that non-state actors would be unable to encroach on what was drastically seen as the government's space" (Riaz & Qureshi, 2017).

In 2002, Ministry of Information and Broadcasting released guidelines for community radio and licenses were restricted to established educational institutions only. Indian government was not willing to liberate its licensing policy and was criticized by activists for continuing dominance and following colonial laws and not letting go of control over media and allowing a third sector to come up along with state controlled and commercially driven media. By 2004, TRAI (Telecom Regulatory Authority of India) was given the power to regulate broadcast. TRAI again had to face criticism as it also preferred to stick to the 2002 policy and continue with the same. A consultation paper of 2004 by TRAI mentioned "The present guidelines permit grant of licenses for setting up Community Radio Stations (CRS) only to educational institutions. Hence community radio licenses are not available to community cooperatives, local self help groups, NGOs, social organisations, trade unions, associations and other non-commercial groups" (Telecom Regulatory Authority of India (TRAI), 2004).

The 2002 community radio policy which was confined to campus radios as popularly known, was only for well established educational institutions to run stations on their campuses with FM transmitters. The policy reduced the hegemony of state but again the radio market went into the hands of, urban, educated, elite coterie in areas that are already well served by media violates the fundamental philosophy behind community radio (Pavarala & Malik, 2007). These campus radio were allowed to air programs on agriculture environment, health and other development related information.

As Saeed, (n.d.) mentions, while the constitutional guarantee as stated in Article 19 (1) (a) of the Freedom of Speech and Expression promises media access to all, the attempts by powerful media houses to colonise the electromagnetic spectrum cannot be denied. Further Saeed (n.d.) says, "while the 'public property theory' could make the task of democratization of CR very easy, coming as it does from the highest court in the country, it fails to explain the ambiguities which exists in the system–Why is 'spectrum' an exclusive property of the government? How are airwaves public properties in a framework where the government has the right to auction, rent, buy or sell frequencies?"

Continuous efforts by activists, NGOs, academicians, individuals and external supporters such as UNESCO and UNDP strengthen the community logic and right to access to airwaves. In May 2004, Ministry of Information and

Broadcasting organised a workshop supported by UNESCO and UNDP to design an enabling framework for Community Radio in India. The workshop brought together a large number of community radio enthusiasts, academics, NGOs and policy makers, who worked out a set of recommendations for a new CR policy, one that would allow community groups to run their own radio stations (Pavarala & Malik, 2007). An online petition campaign by many CR groups was launched subsequently, demanding the inclusion of right of community within CR policy which can end the discrimination against rural and poor communities.

In 2005, Group of Ministers took almost a year to approve the draft policy as they were disagreeable on the issues such as advertising, news and information, license fee, spectrum availability and so on. Finally in 2006, the policy was cleared by the Union Cabinet allowing communities and civil society groups that have been demanding the right to broadcast also be extended to them.

Policy Guidelines for Community Radio in India

In December 2002, Government of India approved a policy for the grant of licenses for setting up of Community Radio Stations (CRS) only in well established educational institutes. In 2006, policy was broad based and it was decided to allow 'Non-profit' organisations like civil society and voluntary organisations etc. under its ambit in order to allow great participation by civil society on issues relating to developing in social change (Community Radio Facilitation Centre (CRFC), Policy Guidelines for setting up Community Radio Stations in India, n.d.)

Highlights of the Community Radio Policy Guidelines

- NGOs, which include voluntary organisations and civil society, State Agriculture Universities (SAUs), ICAR institutions, Krishi Vigyan Kendras, Registered Societies and Autonomous bodies and public trusts registered under societies Act or any other such act relevant for the purpose having at least three years of service.

- The CRs should be designed to serve a specific well defined local community.
- It should have an ownership and management structure that is reflective of the community that the CRS seek to serve.
- The programmes should be of immediate relevance to the community. The emphasis should be on development, agriculture, health, education, environment, social welfare, community development and cultural programs. The programming should reflect the special interest and needs of the local community.
- At least 50% of content shall be generated with the participation of the local community, for which the station has been set up. Programs should preferably be in the local language and dialect (s).

Who cannot apply for CRS

1. Individuals
2. Political parties and affiliated organisations
3. Organisations operating with a motive to earn profit
4. Organisations expressly banned by the Union and State Government

Community Radio Sustainability: Funding and Challenges

Community Radio Stations operate in a defined geographic community. Participation of local community at various level not only fosters a sense of ownership but also make them feel empowered as their voices were never getting any platform from where they can be heard. Once an organisation of civil group get license, it has to look at the revenue generation aspects as it would be the only thing which will make it sustainable in the longer run. Sustainability has been used here for both meaning first in terms of financial self-sufficiency and sustainability of programs (Singh, 2016)

The central tenet of CR is rooted in empowerment and continuing pursuit of basic needs, the rule of law and a better life. The empowerment of all communities to own, operate and finance their own radio station is an ideal that reflects aspirations of independence, self-sufficiency and sustainability (United Nations Educational, Scientific and Cultural Organisation (UNESCO), International Seminar, 2015). Sustainability of CRS does not entirely depend on the financial aspect, it is equally dependent on social, institutional and technological, though finance play a significant role. Unless the community consider itself a part of the the CRS at every level, which is equally very important for CR's sustainability because its core essence is, community radio by the community, for the community and of the community.

UNESCO strongly advocates support for an enabling environment for community media, and in case of community radio post 2015, promotes for democratic participation and sustainable development in an inclusive and pluralistic media landscape in both urban and rural settings. The Indian government has not made any changes in the funding and sustenance part of CRS, the policy is same since 2002.

The relevant Extracts of CR Policy Guidelines Relating to Funding:

Section 8–Funding and Sustenance

1. Applicants will be eligible to seek funding from multilateral aid agencies. Applicants seeking foreign funds for setting up the CRS will have to obtain FCRA clearance under Foreign Contribution Regulation Act, 1976.
2. Transmission of sponsored programs shall not be permitted except programs sponsored by Central & State Governments and other organizations to broadcast public interest information. In addition, limited advertising and announcements relating to local events, local businesses and services and

employment opportunities shall be allowed. The maximum duration of such limited advertising will be restricted to 5 (Five) minutes per hour of broadcast.

3. Revenue generated from advertisement and announcements as per Para 8 (ii) shall be utilized only for the operational expenses and capital expenditure of the CRS. After meeting the full financial needs of the CRS, surplus may with prior written permission of the Ministry of Information & Broadcasting be ploughed into the primary activity of the organization i.e. for education in case of educational institutions and for furthering the primary objectives for which the NGO concerned was established.

(Commonwealth Educational Media Centre for Asia (CEMCA), Ethical Practice Guidelines (EPG), 2013).

Funding is one very distinctive feature of CR apart from its content and ownership. CRs are not commercial radios and as they are serving communities with a motive of development and social change and not for commercial returns. The revenue generation policy is confined within specific norms which emphasis on funding from various sources but primarily, the community served determines the programming. CEMCA (Commonwealth Educational Media Centre for Asia) came out with Ethical Practice Guidlines for Community Radio Stations, also mentions about sponsorship policy.

- Sponsorship will not be a factor in deciding who can access broadcasting time. (This could be done by limiting the proportion of broadcast time that can be dedicated to sponsor programming).
- Ensure editorial decisions affecting the content and style of individual programmes are not influenced by programme or station sponsors.
- Ensure that editorial decisions affecting the content and style of overall station programming are not influenced by programme or station sponsors.

(CEMCA, EPG, 2013)

Talking about financial sustainability of CR stations, experts believed that government funding was not the only way. Dr. R. Sreedher, Consultant, Community Media, Commonwealth Educational Media Centre for Asia (CEMCA), argued that content sustainability was a bigger factor than financial sustainability for Community Radio. "Open your doors to the community and give them a platform to express themselves," he urged (Kumar, 2016). In May 2014 at New Delhi, UNESCO and CEMCA launched a participatory research initiates to explore the sustainability parameters for community radio stations in South Asian regions. Some of the key findings were:

- On the whole, CR stations have been able to develop several mechanisms for community participation, particularly with regard to content creation. However, the proportion of live programmes broadcast at most CR stations is very low.
- Much remains to be done for CR stations to attain financial independence and sustainability. CR stations run by large and medium NGOs have been fairly successful in building financial sustainability. Stations with large parent organizations enjoy greater infrastructural stability, but fear the possible closure of the CR station if the parent organization's support is withdrawn. Stations in remote, resource poor and sparsely populated areas on the other hand would require some form of public funding to diversify their funding sources.
- While gender parity is high at most stations, less than 50 per cent of the stations studied had formally adopted a gender policy. Although women from the community might play a leadership role with respect to the station's day-to-day content and broadcast management, but this is not necessarily the case with respect to financial, technological or institutional decision-making roles. The presence of marginalized community members in staff teams or management

> committees does not always give them a voice in guiding the perspectives of the station's programmes or internal policies. Not all CR stations are able to have open house meetings with their volunteers, and retaining volunteers continues to be a challenge.
>
> (CEMCA, 2015)

Challenges

The challenges to the sustainability of CR range from confusion as to its purpose and role through top-down initiatives that facilitates editorial control by political and commercial interest to an absence of effective policies and fair regulatory practices. The challenges, according to a UNESCO comparative study of more than 30 countries, can occur in the four critical areas of legal, financial, technical and human resource related issues (UNESCO, International Seminar, 2015). Community works on the ethos of pluralistic and independent media, it also promote transparency and demands accountability. It is not a public or commercial media where the editorial control is decided by the state or the market forces. Community radio stations needs to develop a true democratic way of functioning as to have equitable development. The policy has to be in such a form which allow editorial freedom and promote participation from the community.

The general international standards pertaining to community radio require the state to promote media diversity and protect freedom of expression. They serve to inform and assist decision-makers in developing policies and laws to recognize, define and regulate community broadcasting, and their application is crucial to the fostering of pluralism and an enabling environment (UNESCO, International seminar, 2015). It took nearly a decade in India to convince government to understand what community broadcasting means in true sense and the difference between public broadcaster and community broadcaster. Countries like Australia and South Africa legally recognize community broadcasting but country like Chile do not. There are counties like Philippines and

Nepal, who continue to operate without a well defined legislative policy for community radio, but on the contrary Ethiopia does have a policy recently formulated. India has increased its support for this third tier of broadcasting, albeit in an environment where it aspires to the revenue generated by commercial FM radio stations (UNESCO, International seminar 2015).

CR runs on the basic principle of non-profit and has a mission to serve geographically defined communities and communities of interest unlike commercial radio which is profit driven. CR generates revenue to sustain its broadcasting operations, on the other hand commercial radio generate profits for shareholders. CR is dependent upon their co-operatives ownership, NGOs, foreign assistance, national government in case of educational institutions/universities and audience participation.

India has introduced reforms that empower community radio by reducing licensing fees and easing application procedures.

Non-profit organizations and educational institutions are both eligible to operate a station as long as they acquire approval for a license and frequency allocation from the ministries of information and broadcasting and communication and information technology. India also provides public funding through the Community Radio Support Fund administered by the information and broadcasting ministry. The centralized management of the fund has raised concerns about community media becoming an extension of government media (UNESCO International seminar, 2015).

When it comes social sustainability, it becomes the responsibility of CRS to promote participation not only in content generation but at the management, also at agenda setting level. Innovations are possible in this context and a few models can be developed to engage community in decision making in the real sense. Contributions of community volunteers need to be compensated through innovative approaches to continue support and engagement with the CR sector (CEMCA, Ministry of Information and Broadcasting, 2014).

TRAI 2014 Recommendations

Ministry of Information and Broadcasting asked TRAI to recommend mechanism through which the existing and potential CRS could renew their licenses. TRAI came out with a consultation paper to seek views from stakeholders. Several civil organisations, individuals, representative associations and broadcasting radio stations provided their views. It was in 2004, when for the first time TRAI came out with recommendations, and now after a decade for the second time released a set of recommendation on August 2014.

TRAI's recommendation on the issue of license renewal, that incumbent stations can be given renewal for a period of five years, after which extension would be subject to self-evaluation reports that could be verified. It also lays down guidelines for extension of the grant of permission to stations for an additional ten years only if the station is continues operations and permission from district magistrate to shift a station in disaster (Seshu, 2017). TRAI also recommended an e-governance enabled single window mechanism for applicants, since the current process is overly cumbersome and bureaucratic (Pavarala & Bhat, 2014).

TRAI did not try to increase the current advertisement duration of five minutes per hour of broadcast as the finding have shown that radio stations that serves to deprived communities have not been able to utilise the existing five minutes. The limited evidence collected by TRAI indicates that advertising was not able to generate revenues for CRS. Community radio serves majorly to the low income groups who do not have lifestyle for products which are not relevant for them. This reason makes a CRS a very unattractive medium for marketing by the advertisers. As Pavarala & Bhat (2014), finds this recommendation very logical, it signals the need for radically rethinking how CRS can be sustained. Increasing advertising slot cannot bring revenues to CRS as the objective of community is different, it is not market driven. This also brings back the challenges CRS are facing for their sustainability. To encourage self-sustainability and enhance the CRS's relevance to the community, the stipulation that DAVP approved rate are their lowest rates and exclusive to DAVP and cannot be offered any other agency should be relaxed in case of community radio stations (TRAI, consultation paper 2014).

TRAI's recommendations to allowing rebroadcast news from All India Radio and also translate the news into local language, dialect without distorting the content was highly criticized by CR activists as well as media professionals. This came as a surprise for CR promoters as they never asked for it, they have always been voicing for right to broadcast original news - nor acknowledges the transmission of various categories of information as news (Seshu, 2017).

TRAI has reasoned that there is scope for misuse and misleading information may be broadcast in the guise of local news. TRAI also defends its recommendation of rebroadcast of news and not allowing original news by saying that since commercial FM is not allowed to broadcast news it would be unfair to allow new broadcast on CRS. Pavarala & Bhat (2014), finds recommendation as betrayal of trust in communities "if communities can be trusted to operate a FM transmitter and broadcast a wide range of programmes for so many years without any monitoring system, then it is baffling now the same communities may 'misuse' or provide misleading information in the guise of local news".

TRAI's internet based monitoring system set up by Ministry of Information and Broadcasting cannot possibly monitor the content. The TRAI's Electronic Media Monitoring Centre (EMMC) in Delhi, cannot do monitoring of all the CRS programs through online streaming. Many CRSs do not have reliable supply of electricity, broadband internet and uploading audio feed will be hardly possible. CRS broadcast in their local languages and dialects, which will be difficult to

EMMC staff to comprehend and follow. Their is again a more technical flaw as Pavarala & Bhat (2014) point out, "these programs are broadcast on local FM transmitter. By the time someone from EMMC realizes that there is something objectionable, it would be too late. This, monitoring system is in effect post-facto and can (in best of circumstances) be used to provide warnings etc. In no way can the monitoring system prevent misuse". TRAI's denial to give right to broadcast news to CRS because it would be unfair to commercial radio also does not go well with CR supporters. Government does not want to allow broadcast of news to FM stations or CRS, it wants to continue its control on it.

Conclusion

More than two decades back first time the concept of Community Radio was brought up in India. It took more than ten years for CR activists to create a space for this third sector. It was not easy for government to let go of the control and monopoly of radio. This alternative media which emerged world wide from 1970s on wards, created a media space for the excluded groups which emerged as counter publics and questioned the dominant public sphere which was controlled either by the corporate or state media. Active campaigning for three tier broadcast system in India, helped in reducing the gap between media and the people at the grassroots. These excluded group were never represented by mainstream media.

Radio is affordable medium to communicate and can easily meet the information needs of people who have no or low literacy levels. CR is the best form of communication tool when geographically confined region to be served. CRS activists in India have to struggle for quite a long time to make Government of India understand what a community means, and information needs of every community is very different which cannot be met by the mainstream media which is controlled by market forces or state. The government's reluctance to have a third sector also raised questions on its intentions to continue its monopoly in radio.

UNESCO see community radio as a facilitator of democracy, development, independent and pluralistic media. UNESCO, as the only United Nations agency having an authorized mandate to promote media development, has been trying to produce quite a number of indicators and tools which can strengthen the capacity of nations who want to join the movement of development and social change through an effective and participatory two communication.

Community radio is different from other media as its objectives are different, it work on inclusion of society and creating spaces to broaden public debates and strengthen the voice of people who have been ignored by the mainstream media. India and many other countries have formulated policy for community radio, every country in the world have a policy for CR, in fact there is no universal definition of "Community Radio" means that the relevant national legislation varies depending on the country and the multiple strands that define the local context (Unesco, 2015). As CR work with a different intentions to accomplish a different purpose, its sustainability face not only financial challenges but other aspects also play equal role. From ownership of the CRS, to its management, content generation, volunteers to permanent staff all have to be to be from community only. Unless equal participation is witnessed from the community, a CRS cannot sustain. It also means, participation among all classes, ages, no discrimination on the basis of gender or caste or ones literacy levels. The government have to look beyond the advertisements and government funding for the sustainability of CRS.

REFERENCES

Bailur, Savita (2012). Who Is the Community in Community Radio?. *Economic and Political Weekly*, 47 (17), 92-98

CEMCA & Ministry of Information and Broadcasting, (2014). *Innovations in Community Radio with special Reference to India.* Retrieved from www.mib.nic.in/sites/default/Files/innovations_CR_MIB_CEMCA.pdf

CEMCA (2013). *Ethical Practice Guidelines for Community Radio Stations.* Retrieved from www. cemca.org.in/ckfinder/userfiles/files/Low_Res_PG_for_CR.pdf

CEMCA, (2015), *Community Radio and Sustainability A Participatory Research Initiative.* Retrieved from www.unesdoc.unesco.org/images/0023 / 002330/0233084e.pdf

Coyer, Kate & Hintz, Arne (2013). *Media Freedom and Pluralism.* Ed. Klimkiewicz Beata. Budapest: Open Edition Books

CRFC. (n.d.) *Policy Guidlines for setting up Community Radio Stations in India.* Retrieved from www.crfc.in/policy-guidelines-for- setting-up-community-radio-stations-in-india

Kumar, Ashok, (2016). *Holistic sustainability key to Community Radio in India.* Retreived 5, June,2017, from www.southasia.oneworld.net?nes-you-can-use/ press-release/holistic-sustainablity-key-to- community-radio-in-india#.WUD8FWiGM2w

Loeser, H.G. (n.d.). *Community Broadcasting: Publics, Participants and Policies.* Retrieved from http://is.muni.cz/el/1423/jaro2016/ZUR354?um? CB_Book_Ch.6_Community_Broadcasting.pdf

Pavarala, Vinod & Bhat, Ram (2014), *Towards an equitable policy on Community Radio.* Retreived from www.thehindu.com/opinion/open-page/community-radio-in-need-of-an-equitable-policy/ article6394352.ece

Pavarala, Vinod & Malik, Kanchan (2007). *Other Voices The Struggle for Community Radio in India.* New Delhi: Sage Publication

Riaz, Suhaib & Qureshi, Israr (2017), *Emergence.* Ed. Marc-David L. UK: Eneral Publishing

Saeed, Saima. (n.d.) *Community Radio. Policies, Power and Possibilities.* Retrieved from http://community radio.in/pdf/community-radio-policies-power-and possiblities-paper:

Seshu, Geeta,2017,*New policy dismay Community Radio activists.* Retrieved from www.thehoot.org/media-watch/community-media/new-policy-dismays-community-radio-activists-9935

Singh, Ashish (2016). *Self-Sustainablity of Community Radio: Stories from India.* Retrieved June,8,2017, from www.countercurrents.org/2016/08/25/ self-sustainability-of-community-radio-stories-from-India

TRAI. (2004). *Recommendations on Licensing Issues Relating to Community Radio Stations, 9 December 2004.* Retrieved from www.trai.gov.in/sites/ default/files /recom 9 dec.pdf

UNESCO (2015). *International Seminar on Community Media: Sustainability. 14-15 September 2015. Background Paper Community Radio Sustainability Policies and* Funding. Retrieved from www.unesco.org/fileadmin/ MULTIMEDIA/HQ/ci/cipdf/Events cms_sept15_background_paper_en.pdf

7

Community Radio for Empowering Rural Masses in India: Performance and Prospects

Dr. Albert Abraham

1. Introduction

Informed citizenry is a necessary prerequisite for social development in its truest sense. Mass media constitute the largest platform that informs and educates the public on a wide range of social and development issues. For the last two decades, there has been a paradigmatic shift in approach to mass media, as a tool for development and empowering people. Along with advance in media technology, evolution of the very concept of development from quantitative growth to qualitative empowerment and human development has triggered this transition. Earlier, mass media were used for imparting exogenous knowledge to the target audience with a top to bottom approach, having a sender/source bias, assuming that the end beneficiaries of communication are passive receivers. For the first three decades in the post-World War II era, this perspective reined the dominant development communication

Albert Abraham is currently an Assistant Professor of Journalism, in Kamala Nehru College, University of Delhi. He Secured PhD in Community Communication from Faculty of Social Sciences, University of Delhi, Delhi.

paradigm. But, due to its inevitable failure and counter productive effects like information and knowledge divide, this approach has been challenged and alternative and people centric communication paradigms like community newspapers, community radio and community/participatory video were emerged. All these initiatives are categorized under an umbrella terminology 'community media'.

This chapter explores the performance and prospects of non-commercial, non-profit and community based community radio stations in India in empowering the rural masses, by facilitating an alternative and decentralized paradigm of communication for social development.

2. Community Media and the Alternative Development Communication Paradigm

Community media initiatives including community radio belong to the alternative paradigm of development communication, that originated as the outcome of the critique of the earlier dominant and dependency paradigms[1]. The philosophy of alternative paradigm, which is essentially participatory, can be summarized in Fals Borda's words 'people cannot be liberated by a consciousness and knowledge other than their own'[2]. With the works of Everett Rogers and others, participatory and inclusive aspects began to get acceptance in the development discourse and consequently in the theory and practice of development communication.

In 1975, a working group of the International Conference on Communication Policies for Rapidly Developing Societies held at Mashhad in Iran identified detailed activities that development communication must strive for achieving development. They include: determination of the needs of the people and the provision of sufficient citizen access to the communication systems to serve as effective feedback to government; provision of horizontal and vertical (interactive) communication linkages at all levels of society and communication channels through which people at all levels of society and in all regions and localities can communicate with one another in order to accomplish the co-ordination necessary for human and material development; provision of local media to serve as effective communication channels; provision of relevant information; and raising people's awareness of development projects and opportunities, and helping to foster attitudes and motivations that contribute to development. Thus, a participatory communication system in the alternative development paradigm enables communities to diagnose the development problems that they face, make well-informed decisions, mobilize for action, and assume responsibility for their own development.

The debates initiated by McBride Commission[3] in the early 1980s pointed out the critical imbalances in the world information flows and called for a New World Information and Communication Order (NWICO) with greater equity, justice and balanced distribution of communication. Calabrese (2005) observes that the legacy of McBride Report titled 'One World, Many Voices' inspired the new generation of communication rights activists and consequently the community media initiatives across the globe, including community radio, as alternative and participatory media, aiming at bridging the information and communication divide.

With the emergence of globalization in the end of 1980s, elite, commercial and advertising interests began to take control over the communication and media landscape in most of the countries. Consequently, commercialization of news and monopolization of the information and communication infrastructure by the global media conglomerates led to media hegemony. Thereafter, political power structures and ideologies also began to influence the media systems tremendously. These developments resulted in the 'disempowerment' of people by the 'information and communication divide'.

As the ownership patterns changed and commercial interests swept in, media began to influence news and the public opinion process, and thereby manufacturing consent in the public sphere[4] through hiding and highlighting tactics.

This phenomenon is brilliantly dealt in the modern propaganda theory of media, developed by Noam Chomsky and Edward Herman. Chomsky and Herman traces the routes by which money and power are able to filter out the news fit to print, marginalize dissent, and allow the government and dominant private interests to get their messages across to the public. Chomsky and Herman (1988) identified five filters of media – ownership, funding, sourcing, flak (negative criticism) and ideology – through which the political economy influences the modern media systems. According to them, media operates as a business which sells its products to dual customers – other business entities that advertise in media and the public who depends on media for news, information and entertainment. Often the priorities of these dual customers may conflict with each other and subsequently distort the media systems.

According to the Peasants' Charter published in 2014 by FAO, 'Participation by the people in the institutions and systems which govern their lives is a basic human right and also essential realignment of political power in favour of disadvantaged groups and for social and economic development'. Hence, participatory media systems are essentially required for actualizing the ideals of inclusive human development, good governance, democracy and human rights. Participatory communication envisions the empowerment of individuals and communities by facilitating reciprocal information flow between the senders and the receivers. It advocates for decentralization of the information systems and knowledge economy. People the real beneficiaries of development are involved in schematizing and implementing the grassroot communication systems. Low cost technologies such as low-power VHF, FM radio, camcorders, desk-top publishing and the Internet open up opportunities for people to be in charge of their own communication. In the participatory model, communication is a process, not a series of finished products.

In participatory communication, four ways of participation are identified - participation in decision making, implementation, benefits and evaluation. Participatory communication involves the participation of the people or community in the communication need analysis in the context of development, formulating communication strategies and deciding on communication packages. Participatory communication is inherently inclusive giving equal emphasis on the needs and voices of all segments of the people and respecting the plurality of the society. Community radio stations, community newspapers, participatory video units and user generated contents in the New and Social Media are examples of this alternative paradigm, where the users also become 'produsers'[5] and they also participate in the communication effects analysis and the course corrections required.

3. The Development Communication Paradigm in India: A Critical Appraisal

More than two centuries of the colonial rule had left Indians with a low level economic progress and social development, apart from unimaginable exploitation of human and natural resources. In the post independence scenario, population explosion, corruption, inefficiency in the governance systems and popular indifference to adopt innovation and technology slowed down the developmental initiatives. Hence the relevance of development communication has been significantly increased in the Indian context since independence.

If the media landscape in India for the last seventy years is subtly analyzed, it is clear that mass media - particularly Radio and Television - was mainly used for development, modelling the modernization paradigm of the dominant discourse. The monopoly of All India Radio and Doordarshan also slowed down the development communication initiatives, as development continued to be a state agenda and such efforts were struck with administrative and bureaucratic hurdles. This vicious scenario inevitably led to a huge information and knowledge divide in India particularly in rural areas.

Researchers have shown that using mass media for development is also the least effective in ensuring intelligent understanding and effectiveness of development messages (Heshmat, 1967 and Moemeka, 1987). In this method, programs/messages are planned, produced and disseminated by 'experts' and program officers in the urban headquarters of media organizations with very little or no reference to the views and opinions of the receiving audiences. Development messages are planned and executed without consultation with the audiences to whom the messages are originally intended, rendering the communication package with a little chance of succeeding.

Also, it has to be noticed that the iconic development communication projects undertaken in India, in the earlier decades, like SITE - Satellite Instructional Television Experiment (1975-76), Kheda Communication Project (1975-90), and Jhabua Development Communication Project (mid-1990s) were community based, local, participatory and followed the spirit of narrowcasting. But in course of time, the development communication efforts in India lost this participatory and communitarian vigour and preferred to go passionately for broadcasting the development issues to the masses using public broadcasters. It is important to mention that participatory communication initiatives - the most suitable communication model for development in India, considering the geographical and demographical vastness as well as cultural diversity of the country - got acceptance just a decade ago. Now the role of community media including community radio stations has become crucial in development communication and to revolutionize the media landscape in India.

As a result of corporatization, media in India primarily serve the elite interests in terms of selection/filtering and distribution of news. Most of the development issues covered in Indian media gets their space due to their commercial news value than the development values. The mainstream visual media is shying away from the big responsibility of focusing on such hard but real life issues. The mass media, which is expected to act as a catalyst for development, seems to have forgotten their role and seems contented with their vertical and horizontal growth, thereby ignoring the larger part of the population living in the rural areas. Now the prime focus of media houses in India is on market and readership/viewership rating with the intention to increase the advertising revenue. Profiteering by any means has now become a generally accepted model in the media business. Competition among the different TV channels jams the coherent public opinion building on crucial issues of national or regional importance and development gets a back seat (B.K. Ravi, 2012). As P Sainath (2007) rightly observed, 'the fundamental characteristic of our media is the growing disconnect between mass media and mass reality'.

4. Community Radio Movement in India

The broadcasting scenario has radically changed in India with the arrival of private FM stations, which redefined the entire broadcasting market in the sub-continent. The Ministry of Information and Broadcasting (MIB) began to auction radio frequencies to private players who wanted to start their own commercial and private FM stations, following a landmark judgment by the Supreme Court in 1995 in the case – Cricket Association of Bengal Vs Secretary, Ministry of Information and Broadcasting, Government of India. The judgment, in essence, stated that airwaves are public property and must be used for the public good asserting the fundamental right to freedom of speech and expression enshrined in Article 19 (1)a of the Constitution of India and also in the Universal Declaration of Human Rights (1948).

The Supreme Court judgement augmented the demands of the civil society movements to campaign for and start prototypes of community radio stations across the country using FM technology. Immediately after the Supreme Court judgment, civil society groups formulated the Bangalore Declaration[6], articulating the need for a third tier of broadcasting, i.e. community radio. This was followed up by the Pastapur Declaration[7] in 2000 which re-articulated the need for community radio and also asserted that it ought to be non-profit making, localized and community owned. These two advocacy measures played an important role in the community radio movement in India. Between 1999 and 2001, several community radio initiatives were launched in Karnataka (*Namma Dhwani*), Andhra Pradesh (*Sangam* Radio), Jharkhand (*Chala Ho Gaon Mein*) and Gujarat (Radio *Ujjas*), which used either cable radio or bought time slots on AIR to broadcast the local contents.

Until late 2006, only educational institutions were allowed to set up community radio stations having a transmission range of 10-15 km under strict conditions. *Anna* FM is India's first campus 'community' radio, launched on 1st February 2004, controlled by an education and multimedia research centre in Anna University. Later, organizations like Voices[8] and *Drishti* Media[9] introduced an innovative practice called narrowcasting to circumvent the policy restrictions. They worked with NGOs at Bangalore and in Gujarat to train community reporters to produce radio programs, the programs being played out over loudspeakers in common community meeting points such as temples and *panchayat* meetings, or within 'listener groups' of women in self-help groups.

The spectacular success of these experiments in empowering communities prompted enterprising activists from other non-profit organizations to lobby for a liberal policy for community radio broadcasting. The Government of India declared a community radio policy in 2004, but it defined 'communities' rather narrowly to include only educational institutions. The exclusion of grassroots communities somewhat defeated the very purpose of the legislation. On 16 November 2006, the Government of India issued a set of new community radio guidelines which expanded the scope of organization and entitled non-profit agencies, agricultural research institutes and registered societies/autonomous bodies/public trusts to set-up community radio stations using the FM band 88–108 MHz.

These radio stations are expected to produce at least 50 per cent of their programs in the local range and the programs should be presented in the local language or dialect to the maximum extent. Their prime focus would be on developmental programming, though there is no clear restriction on entertainment. The subsequent policy changes allowed some new categories of news and varied forms of communication that are permitted including sports news and commentaries, information on traffic and weather conditions, coverage of cultural events and festivals, information on educational events, civic announcement's adhering to the utilities like electricity, water supply, disaster warnings, and health alerts.

According to the Ministry of Information and Broadcasting (MIB), there are 200 community radio stations are functional now and about 4,000 community radio licenses have been on offer across India. As on 01 November 2016, grant of permission was awarded to 252 applicants and letter of intent were given to 449 applicants, from various educational institutions, NGOs, *Krishi Vigyan Kendra* and State Agriculture Universities among 1930 applicants (accessed from www.mib.nic.in on 30 May 2016).

5. Community Radio Stations in India: Case Studies

In order to understand the organizational, functional and development communication aspects of community radio stations in India, two case studies of Radio *Mattoli* and Radio *Dhadkan* are made.

5.1. Radio Mattoli 90.4 FM

Radio *Mattoli* 90.4 FM established on 01 July 2009 is Kerala's first Community Radio station situated at Dwaraka (Mananthavady) in Wayanad primarily a hilly agrarian district. Radio *Mattoli* owned and operated by Wayanad Social Service Society (WSSS) covers all 49 villages of the district and reaches to a population of 8.15 lakhs,which comprises farmers, tribals and dalits. It is Kerala's only electronic media that broadcasts programs in tribal dialects daily. It broadcasts 17 hours of programs daily from 06:00 am to 11:00 pm and has approximately 2.5 lakhs listeners. Now radio *Mattoli* makes online streaming of radio programs (similar to internet radio) through its website http://radiomattoli.com/.

The major objectives of Radio *Mattoli* are: to create an alternate and sustainable communication system for free flow of information, to penetrate all the sections with a special focus on the alienated communities, to reflect people's opinions, enhance socio-economic conditions in the villages, to become the voice of the voiceless, to enhance cultural, political and artistic voices of these communities, to sustain biodiversity, transform community life, highlight localized issues, news and culture, and to foster women's participation. Editorial management of *Mattoli* vests with a committee consisting of volunteers representing different sections of the society. Around 20 volunteers are selected from the community and given training for knowledge and skills pertaining to radio broadcasting and programming. They constantly interact with the people and understand the development issues to be covered in the community radio programs.

The financial sustenance of Radio *Mattoli* is through projects and funds from various Government Agencies like – National Bank for Agriculture and Rural Development (NABARD); Agricultural Technology Management Agency (ATMA); Department of Science & Technology and Ministry of Panchayati Raj, Government of India; Ministry of Culture and Ministry of Health & Family Welfare, Government of Kerala, National Human Rights Commission (NHRC), Indian Coffee Board, Indian Spices Board, Rajiv Gandhi National Institute of Youth Development (RGNIYD), Tribal Development Department, Kerala State Legal Service Authority (KELSA), National Rural Health Mission (NRHM), and NGOs etc. Radio *Mattoli* also receives advertisements from Directorate of Audio Visual Publicity (DAVP), Public Relations Department, Government of Kerala and local advertisers.

Programming

Radio *Mattoli*'s programs cover a range of issues of education, culture, health, environment, agriculture, animal husbandry and community development. Programs are aired in Malayalam and four indigenous tribal dialects – *Paniya, Kurichiya, Kuruma* and *Urula*. The programs are educational in substance as they intend to empower people through participatory media and democratization of knowledge and information.

A selected list of programs having implications of social development is given below.

- *Arogyavedi* (health forum) telecasts health and hygiene related programs.
- Career *Mattoli* focuses on employment issues for youth, along with introducing new skill development courses and training for them.
- *Jan Vaani* (People's Voice) is a program that brings in an open platform to freely discuss various socio-political and economic issues and thereby creating informed public opinion through dialogue.
- *Karimani* is a program for empowerment of tribal women.
- *Ksheeravaani* is a program for dairy farmers.
- *Kudumbavedi* (family forum) contains programs promoting health and family welfare.
- *Letter Box* is a fortnightly program based on feedbacks of the listeners, gauging its participatory approach in the contents generation and evaluation of the programs.
- *Mattoli Talkies* and *Arangu* contain locally relevant entertainment programs.
- *Niyamavum Neethiyum* (law and justice) is a legal literacy program.
- *Njangalkkumunduparayaan* (We also have to say) provides people an opportunity to present development issues from their perspectives.
- *Njattuvela* contains programs for farmers.
- *Thudi Chetham* is a program made by *adivasi* (tribal) volunteers in tribal dialects and dealing with a wide range of tribal issues.

- *Unarav* helps the tribal people to express their culture, knowledge and traditions and thereby asserting the social and cultural identity of the tribal groups.
- *Vanitha Mattoli* is an exclusive program for women empowerment made by women volunteers. It deals with issues such as domestic violence, income generating activities for women, education of girl children etc.
- *Vayalnaadu* is an agricultural extension program supported by ATMA.
- *Vijnaanavedhi* contains informational and educational programs.
- *Yuvatharangam* consists of programs for youth.
- *Thangum Thanalum* is a financial literacy programs supported by NABARD.

Impacts

Radio *Mattoli* has given greater visibility, recognition and respect to tribal dialects, culture and identity. As a result, for the first time in the Kerala's history, electioneering was done in tribal dialects in Wayanad District, during the Panchayath Elections of 2010. This trend continued during the consecutive Legislative Assembly Elections (2011 & 2016) and General Elections (2014). Radio *Mattoli* could decisively engage in civil grievances and their redressal though participation of complainants and civil authorities, which benefitted the larger society in many respects. The greatest impact Radio *Mattoli* could make is formation of *Mattoli* School Clubs in around 100 schools which provide opportunities for the students to listen to the community radio programs and enable them to make their own radio programs. By receiving the National Community Radio awards for Sustainability and Programming in the consecutive years since 2012, Radio *Mattoli* has proven its prowess in transforming the community media landscape in Kerala. From the programming practices, it is clear that Radio *Mattoli* promotes participatory, inclusive and grassroots level radio broadcasting and thereby educating and empowering people on various social and development issues.

5.2. Radio Dhadkan 107.8 FM

The United Nations Children's Fund (UNICEF) collaborated with an NGO *Sambhav* to set up a community radio station called 'Radio *Dhadkan*' (RD) in Shivpuri district in Madhya Pradesh in 2010. The arrival of Radio *Dhadkan* (RD) transformed the region as it could effectively raise people's voice against gender and caste based discrimination prevalent there. The launch of Radio *Dhadkan* marked the beginning of a battle against social evils and empowering women especially the *Sahariya* tribal women. Covering 71 villages in the Chambal region of Madhya Pradesh, with 12 hours program per day, its core strategy is to utilize the scope of community communication for catering to the rural information needs and thereby promoting community development and empowerment.

Radio *Dhadkan* started narrowcasting in November 2008. Till October 2010, it was mainly engaged in program development, narrowcasting and capacity building of the volunteers. The RD volunteers organized around 300 listener group meetings and narrowcasting sessions in targeted villages and sub-urban areas in Shivpuri. In 2010, RD commenced community broadcasting that widened its reach considerably. Since its inception, RD has covered a population of over 1.7 lakhs, of which two-third constitute marginalized communities - i.e. 20.3% Scheduled Caste, 8% percent Scheduled Tribe, and 43.7% Other Backward Communities, according to the Census Data, 2011).

Programming

Programs in Radio *Dhadkan* focus on healthcare and hygiene, breast feeding and neo-natal care, prevention and cure of HIV/ AIDS, conservation of water and land resources, agriculture and livelihood issues, and education of girl children - the key issues pertinent to the region. The programs also facilitate literacy efforts, skill development and career options for the youth, various government schemes for development, conservation of *Sahariyya* tribal dialect and folk culture.

In order to ensure optimum participation of people from the *Sahariya* community, the following measures have been undertaken: organization of listener group meetings every month, conducting narrowcasting sessions in the targeted villages, deploying adolescent girls along with other villagers as volunteers, collusion of the whole community in the operation of theme selection, content development, production and finalization of programs, creating awareness and empowering the marginalized through home to home workshops, recruiting volunteers from within villages and training them in script writing, recording, editing and other operational aspects and conducting meetings to elicit feedback on the programs being offered.

Important Programs produced and telecasted by Radio *Dhadkan* are:

- Programs promoting key-flagship development schemes like Mahatma Gandhi National Rural Employment Guarantee Act (MNREGA), Total Sanitation Campaign (TSC), National Rural Health Mission (NRHM) and *Sarva Shiksha Abhiyan* (SSA).
- *Shivpuri Atit se Aaj Tak* promotes programs on folk culture.
- Programs on female infanticide and feticide.
- *Bal Jagat* is a portrayal of key issues through poems, songs and stories for children.
- *Rozgaar Mantra* is a program on youth employment.
- *Swadisht Vyanjan,* is a food based program focusing on nutrition.

Impacts

Being an offshoot of UNICEF'S millennium development goals (MDGs) Radio *Dhadkan* has showcased itself as a strong people's media with the following impacts.

- There has been significant enhancement in the knowledge level of people, regarding personal and public hygiene, immunization and other healthy practices in the community.

- RD could facilitate dialogue for development at the grassroot level. People now share their problems on this open forum, either through volunteers or utilizing feedback mechanisms. Radio *Dhadkan* promotes participation and empowerment of people for materializing inclusive development goals.
- RD gives voice to marginalized, particularly tribal population and women. Tribal people have started availing benefits of the government schemes, ever since they started knowing about them. There have been positive signs of women empowerment, particularly among the tribals. Story of Ramavati, a community radio volunteer with Radio *Dhadkan* is inspiring. Six years working in radio gave her the confidence to successfully contest the local elections as an independent candidate, taking radio as her election symbol. Radio transformed her from an ordinary housewife into a village celebrity.
- Preserving *Sahariya*'s cultural heritage through radio programs which could function as digital archives.
- The programs have encouraged people to educate themselves, which has resulted in the decline of illiteracy, and to avail modern medicine and health facilities.
- Resulted in volunteer training and capacity building, and mobilizing collective action for local, inclusive and participatory development.
- Narrowcasting provides access to radio programs in areas where acute communication infrastructure deficiency persists. Each month, field reporters' targets include six narrowcasts and six listener group meetings per village. Getting direct feedback from the communities is an added benefit of narrowcasting.

The growth of community radio in India's rural areas like Wayanad and Shivpuri has been instrumental to revolutionize and democratize information flows in regions long neglected.

Issues pertaining to agriculture, healthcare and hygiene, empowerment of women and maternal health, human rights and livelihood issues are broadcast in local languages and dialects, offering a vital source of education and empowerment for the marginalized segments of the society. From the above detailed deliberations, it can be inferred that the 'community made and community owned' radio stations and their programs undoubtedly promote local cultural heritage, participatory communication and inclusive development.

6. Why Community Radio Matters in India?

Community radio has a rich legacy of challenging dominant discourses in media, airing alternative perspectives, and amplifying the voices of people who are marginalized in the contemporary communications systems. Community radio stations with a participatory approach allow people to produce and distribute media contents tailored to their own needs. It provides tools of participatory communication into the handsof communities for cultural expression, local news and information, contextualized views and educative dialogue, thereby empowering people at the local level.

In India, the 'information and communication divide' is comparatively larger in rural areas. This divide also persists within the rural population–between the rich and the poor, the educated and the illiterate. The information and communication divide occurs due to two major reasons - illiteracy and poor information and communication infrastructure. Illiterate population may not be able to access the communication infrastructure and avail information services. It may reinforce various shades of illiteracy reciprocally. To bridge this divide, accessible and people centric information and communication infrastructure like community radio needs to be promoted.

Community radio can trigger empowerment and social development in rural India, considering the following factors.

6.1. Community Radio as a Suitable Medium for Community Communication

Considering the peculiar socio-economic and cultural conditions and the widespread 'information and knowledge divide' in the South Asian counters, radio can be the most suitable medium to make people's life better. Community radio stations can play a crucial role in this regard, by promoting participation of the poor and deprived rural communities. According to World Association of Community Broadcasters – AMARC[10], the philosophy of community radio is to use radio as the voice of the voiceless and a tool for empowerment and social development.

In communities with high levels of illiteracy and poverty, radio is the most effective and affordable medium which helps to catalyze social change (Girard, 1992 & Dagron, 2001). Since radio uses spoken word, it can overcome the barriers of illiteracy as well as people's general disinterest to read printed materials. People can perform their daily chores while listening to radio programs. Rockefeller Foundation Report (2011) asserts that community radio is 'one of the best ways to reach the excluded or marginalized communities in targeted, useful ways'. Community Radio gives people a 'voice' that matters most in development communication (Dagron, 2001).

According to the Declaration of Principle of Community Radio, by AMARC, "Community radio responds to the needs of the community it serves, contributing to its development within progressive perspectives in favour of social change. Community radio strives to democratize communication through community participation in different forms in accordance with each specific social context'. Community Radio stations use technologies which are appropriate and affordable and reach out to the most remote communities".

The principal stakeholder in a community radio is the community itself and this allows the station to have the discretion to make programs on locally relevant development issues and entertainment. The process of community radio is to bring people together and generate enthusiasm within the community itself. It reminds the community of their responsibilities and pushes the community to progress and develop in a positive way. According to Paolo Freire's educational philosophy, people liberate themselves in collaboration with fellow beings. For that collaboration, meaningful communication is a must and which may be effectively facilitated by community media initiatives like community radio stations.

6.2. Community Radio Facilitates Participatory Communication

Community radio initiatives are collective and participatory in nature. A community radio station acts as a platform to streamline people centric and participatory communication for inclusive development, specific to the geographical and demographic areas in which they operate. The driving force of a community radio station is its active participation of people in producing media contents along with inclusion of locally and culturally relevant information, knowledge and entertainment. The greatest advantage of community radio is that it covers local development issues from the perspectives of rural people, independent of any governmental or commercial interests. In short it is 'a radio of the people, by the people and for the people'. Officials from revenue and health departments, lower bureaucracy and local government are also invited for the community radio programs. This fair approach can expose the differences in the narratives of the people and the authorities and people can have a judgment on such occurrences weighing the reasons from both the sides.

In community media, people decide the topics or issues, make the script, record and edit the programs and telecast/ podcast them. Community media redefines the notion of 'editorial', since the editorial functions of mainstream media are reversed here. Through genuine social intervention, editorial ideas are crowd-sourced and it democratizes the editorial functions. This mechanism immensely empowers people as it gives voice to the voiceless. People become active participants or creators of their own narratives rather than passive spectators of 'otherly' narratives about them.

Community radio facilitates democratization of the information and communication sphere. Community radio, through participatory communication processes contributes to building citizenship and individual participation in the public and democratic sphere. Community radio provides opportunities for the people to hear and to be heard. Involvement and participation of the downtrodden is essential for an effective communication strategy for development.

6.3. Community Radio as an Effective Development Medium

Community radio programs cover a variety of issues - empowerment of the subaltern groups, farmers, dalits, tribal, women, children etc., poor infrastructure in healthcare, transportation, education and communication, lapse in various social development schemes by state and central governments, violation of legal and human rights, corruption and inefficiency in public administration, shortage/absenteeism of health care and public service professionals and teachers, discrepancies in Public Distribution System, poor implementation of relief packages, environmental impacts of infrastructure development and tourism and social evils like crime, alcoholism, drug abuse, child marriage, domestic violence etc.

6.4. Community Radio Enables Communication in the Cultural Context

Community radio helps in preserving local language and cultural expressions, giving additional value to them, and leading to the amelioration of the self-esteem of the community and wide recognition from people outside the community. As Pitabas Pradhan (2011) pointed out, community radio can also reinforce traditional forms of communication such as storytelling, group discussion and theatre and they can enable grassroots participationin policy-making and democracy. For several cultural and linguistic minorities, community radio is the only place where their language is heard and their music being heard and their cultural distinctions are celebrated (Pitabas Pradhan, 2011).

Community radio with the magic of sound can help the survival of local knowledge and reinforce solidarity in the communities, because it attracts the listeners in their own language and can send their messageas the people of the community is producing the programs; it builds ownership that a commercial media could not have. Community radio programs generally carry local language/dialect and symbols rooted in the socio cultural ethos of the respective communities. Using more local examples, simple vocabulary, short sentences, colloquial and conversational language/ dialect, community radio stations ensure that the messages are reached to and understood by the target audience. Also, community radio programs in effect digitize the cultural forms and products in audio format, which could be preserved and accessed.

6.5. Community Radio Facilitates Subaltern Discourse

In a critical analysis of the contemporary mainstream media scenario in India - Print and Broadcast, it is clear that they are owned and controlled by social elites. The subaltern groups like *dalits*, tribal population, lower segments of the society, urban poor, workers,women, and ethnic, religious, gender and linguistic minorities, and their interests are marginalized and even misrepresented in the present media landscape. To resolve this divide, participation of these subaltern groups in the communication process - production and distribution of media narratives, is to be ensured.

There is a significant amount of participation by people from subaltern sections of the society - tribal, *dalit* and women in program production for community radio stations in India. Participation in community radio enables them to be media literate and technology savvy. Programs are anchored by people from such social groups and they can direct the course of the program with a 'subaltern perspective'. Illiterate community radio volunteers assert that illiteracy is not a constraint in participating in community radio and understanding the development issues particularly if they are local specific. Neo-literates also participate largely in program production for community radio stations. Also, community radio stations provide them a sustainable and reasonably paid employment.

Community radio initiatives give opportunities for women's participation and can generate a counter discourse on low participation of women in mainstream media and misrepresentation of women, acknowledging women as agents of development and development communication. Community radio stations empower women by enabling them to participate in the communication process and giving them identity and voice in the public sphere. Also community radio stations help women and other subaltern groups to explore their latent artistic talents.

6.6. Community Radio Promotes Volunteerism and Community Journalism

Community radio programs are made by volunteers from the community modelling a decentralized and participatory communication process. Hence they are the narratives of the community rather than the narratives about the community. Making community radio programs in effect is a research process and a social action that involves community radio volunteers, people from the beneficiary communities and their socio-cultural and development contexts.

Community radio volunteers are given continuous training in scripting, program production and research on development issues, through workshops and colloquiums. Community radio volunteers conduct preliminary research to understand the audience and identify the local development problems. They take feedback and people's opinion into account and thereby the programs in their final shape reflect the aspirations of the people. In order to reach the areas where community radio signals are not available, volunteers carry radio programs and play them in public gatherings. This narrowcasting is highly effective and can be used for instant feedback of the programs.

Training scores of community radio volunteers - most of them are illiterate or neo literate, poor adolescent girls and boys, men and women, community media organizations or promoters could establish a strong and sustainable foundation, which is rural, participatory and democratic in essence. Thus, in this radically changed information and media scenario, everyone acquires the potential to become a (citizen) journalist, a social activist and a vigilant public conscience to make his/her own credible narratives. In community radio programs, banking on the experience and traditional knowledge through prior learning, people become 'subject experts' and it challenges the conventional notion that 'subject experts belong to a quantitatively qualified category of people'.

6.7. Community Radio Programs are Compatible with New/Social Media

New Media Technology can enhance the process and contents of community radio. Penetration of internet and mobile telephony in the rural areas is accelerated than never before in India. In the larger development spectrum, the development issues need to be noticed by the governments, bureaucratic structures, policy think tanks and NGOs. Through social media like Facebook and twitter, volunteers can make the presence of community radio in the digital or online space by sharing them with short descriptions, which may influence the development discourse in the governance and policy forums.

Podcasts and online streaming are used for promoting community radio and making its contents globally available. Further internet based communication platforms and file transfer protocols make the communication between the volunteers and other community radio stations easier, cheaper and faster. Radio on mobile phones not only increased the reach of the community radio programs and audience base, but also it promotes interactivity between people and radio stations. Mobile phones can also be used as a portable audio recording device. Now, programs are shared using mobile applications like WhatsApp. Therefore, systematic and strategic use of new or social media can improve the reach and effectiveness community radio.

6.8. Community Radio Promotes Media Literacy

By demystifying media production techniques, community radio promotes media literacy that imparts knowledge of how production of messages and reproduction of meanings occur and the impact of media on everyday lives of the people. A media literate person is capable of analyzing practices of conventional mainstream media and decoding stereotypes, ideology and cultural pedagogy explicit and implicit in media narratives, which are basically social constructs. Media literacy thus empowers people to use media intelligently, to critically dissect media contents, and to investigate into media uses and effects. Media literacy not only assures quality media consumption opportunities, but also bridges the information and communication divide.

6.9. Community Radio Initiates a Counter Discourse to the Mainstream Media

Community radio being part of the third sector broadcasting generates counter discourse to both public and private sector media by producing programs on local development issues from the perspectives of people, independent of any governmental or commercial interests. Time and space are the major constraints in conventional mainstream media (Newspapers, TV and Radio), while alternatives like community radio initiatives can cover more local development issues. Community radio can supplement the efforts of mainstream media in the development discourse and bridge the gap left by mainstream media, particularly in covering issues like corruption, inefficiency and discrepancy in implementing social development projects and schemes, violations of gender and human rights, and the issues pertaining to land rights of the poor and the tribal along with agriculture, environment and infrastructure development etc. Since community radio stations are not influenced by government and commercial interests, they enjoy more 'editorial freedom' comparing to public and commercial radio broadcasting.

7. Conclusion

In the new and alternative media landscape, community radio initiatives with participatory and inclusive perspectives to communication, reversed the dominant top to bottom approach and devised an audience centric communication paradigm. Community radio narratives are made by people with the assistance of the community radio volunteers, based on the precise understanding of development needs in their context, than the external conception of development and communication practices. Inclusion of local dialects, cultural contents and *voxpopuli* (people's voice) in community radio programs gives a sense of belongingness to people and makes the message simple and easy to understand. In this new communication or media paradigm, people are no more passive beneficiaries, they are the active participants of communication and development, and thereby creators of their own destiny.

Community radio democratizes the media economy by balancing the information flow and compensating the time constraints of the public and private radio broadcasting. In the process, community radio demystifies the 'seemingly complicated radio production techniques' and promote media literacy. These subaltern and counter media narratives (as people from the marginalized sections largely participate in community radio) envisioning a decentralized media landscape could make radical changes at the grassroots and empower people. Community radio makes 'own narratives by people' than 'narratives about people by others'.

End Notes

1. Dependency paradigm emerged as a reaction to Modernization theory (dominant paradigm) of development which held that all societies progress through similar stages of development and adapting exogenous knowledge and technology. Dependency theory argued that resource flow from poor underdeveloped countries (periphery nations) to the rich developed countries (core nations) enriched the latter and therefore their development is dependent on or at the cost of the underdeveloped countries.
2. Orlando Fals Borda was a Columbian sociologist and one of the proponents of Participatory Action Research (PAR) - an approach to research in communities, that stresses participation and action, and emphasizes collective enquiry and experimentation.
3. McBride commission was a 16 member UNESCO panel set up in 1977 and chaired by Nobel Peace Prize laureate Sean MacBride to study communication problems particularly in the developing world.
4. Public Sphere - a term coined by German philosopher Jürgen Habermas means a social space where individuals can freely discuss and identify societal problems, and influence political action. Virtual Public Sphere is the extension of the public sphere to the digital/social media space.
5. 'Produser' – combining user and producer – is a term originated from 'produsage' a concept developed by Australian media scholar Axel Bruns. It refers to user led content creation.
6. Bangalore Declaration - Policy planners, media professionals and Community Based Organizations gathered in Bangalore in September 1996 to study how community radio could be relevant in India. A 'Bangalore Declaration' was signed, and since then it had become the foundation of advocacy for community radio station in India.
7. Pastapur Declaration - A UNESCO sponsored workshop from 17 to 20, July 2000 in Hyderabad and Pastapur (Andhra Pradesh) brought out the 'Pastapur Initiative on Community Radio', urging the government to create a three-tier structure of broadcasting in India - state-owned public radio, private commercial radio, and a non-profit community radio.
8. Voices – is a Bangalore based NGO which set up India's first community based radio station – *Namma Dhwani* (Our Voice) in Bodhikote (Karnataka) in collaboration with MYRADA (another NGO established in 1968) and UNESCO.

9. *Drishti* Media – a Development Communication NGO founded in 1993 in Ahmedabad, Gujarat.
10. AMARC - *Association Mondiale Des Radiodiffuseurs Communautaires* - World Association of Community Radio Broadcasters is an international NGO established in 1983 in Montreal that serves community radio movement with around 4000 associates spread across 130 countries.

REFERENCES

Calabrese, Andrew. (2005). The Promise of Civil Society: A Global Movement for Communication Rights. *Continuum: Journal of Media and Cultural Studies* 18(3).

Dagron, Gumucio, A. (2001): Making Waves: Stories of Participatory Communication for Social Change: A Report to the Rockefeller Foundation. New York: Rockefeller Foundation.

Fraser, C., and Estrada, S.R. (2001). Community Radio Handbook. Paris: UNESCO.

Freire, Paulo. (1970). Pedagogy of the Oppressed. New York: The Seabury Press.

Girard, B. (1992): A Passion for Radio: Radio Waves and Community. Montréal: Black Rose Books.

Ground Realities: Community Radio in India. (2011). New Delhi: UNESCO.

Herman, Edward S. and Noam Chomsky. (1988). Manufacturing Consent: The Political Economy of the Mass Media. New York: Pantheon.

Heshmat, M.Y. (1967). The Role of Radio in Health Education of the Public. *Medical Annals*, Vol. 36 (11).

Jacobson, T. and J. Servaes (Eds.). (1999). Theoretical Approaches to Participatory Communication. New Jersey: Hampton Press.

Kumar, Kanchan. (2003). Mixed Signals: Radio Broadcasting Policy in India. Economic and Political Weekly, Vol. XXXVIII, No. 22.

Moemeka, Andrew A. (1987). Rural Radio Broadcasting and Community Health Practices in Nigeria: A Case-Study of Radio O-Y-O. Albany: State University of New York.

Pavarala, Vinod. (2007). Other Voices: The Struggle for Community Radio in India. New Delhi: Sage Publications.

Pradhan, Pitabas. (2011). Community Radio as an Alternative Tier of Broadcasting: The Challenges and Prospects in India. *Media Watch* Vol. 2 No. 1.

Policy Guidelines for Setting up Community Radio Stations in India. (2006). Ministry of Information & Broadcasting, Govt. of India.

Ravi, B.K. (2012). Media and Social Responsibility: a Critical Perspective with Special Reference to Television. *Academic Research International*. Vol. 2. No. 1.

Rogers, E.M. (1962). Diffusion of Innovations. New York: Free Press.

Sainath, P. (2007, November 13, 14 & 15). Three Part Article on Farmers' Suicides. *The Hindu*.

Srampickal, S.J. (2006). Development and Participatory Communication. Communication Research Trends,Vol.25 (2). Rome: Pontificia Università Gregoriana.

Sreedher, R. et al. (2012). Abiding Voices: Sustainability of Community Radio in India. New Delhi: Commonwealth Educational Media Centre for Asia (CEMCA).

Tufte, Thomas and Mefalopulos, Paolo. (2009). Participatory Communication: A Practical Guide Washington DC: World Bank.

8

Radio–The Evergreen Medium

Dr. Abhijit Bora

"Radio is a combination of the schoolhouse, the church, the public rostrum, the newspaper, the theatre, the concert hall - in fact, all media devoted to education, enlightenment, and education of people. Also, it claims a more intimate relationship with the public than any other medium or tool of information at any given time," Anning S Paul, the first Chief Commissioner of the Federal Communications Commission of the USA in 1936.

"The Press is the best instrument for enlightening the mind of man, and improving him as a rational, moral and social being," Thomas Jefferson, President of the USA (1801-09).

Radio is the oldest of the electronic media with a history of public service broadcasting stretching for more than 80 years now. But, at a time of considerable growth and development of media in general Radio's importance is being tended to be undervalued by the people concerned.

The purpose of broadcasting media is not merely to disseminate plain information or entertain superficially. These

Professor & Head, Department of Mass Communication & Journalism
Tezpur University, Napaam, Tezpur- 784028, Sonitpur (Assam)

are tools, weapons for social development. Hence this medium must be used for public welfare, creative and interactive public tools. For the majority of the world population, particularly by those belonging to disadvantaged groups, radio and television remain the most accessible and widespread means of information and communication. Radio continues to be the most widely accessible communication medium. UNESCO is committed to promote Public Service Broadcasting (PSB) and empower citizens with knowledge to participate actively in decision-making process. (Khan, 2005).

Further, the Extension, Education and Communication Service of Food and Agricultural Organization (FAO) summarizes the most important functions of rural radio as – a tool for democratization, a platform for the expression of ideas and opinions, an alternative media to the imperfections of public and commercial media, a conflict management tool, an agent of social change, a channel for the diffusion of information on rural issues, a tool that can be used for training and the transfer and exchange of knowledge and technologies, a channel for interactive communication, dialogue and debate on the major issues of rural development, a medium to collect local information on social issues which is essential for defining, planning and implementing local development efforts, a tool for cultural expression and entertainment, and a means of collecting, preserving and promoting the oral and musical heritage of rural communities, a tool for social investigation.

These statements reaffirm the immensely-potential scope of radio as the perfect medium for mass communication. Specially for nations like that of India where major portion of world's illiterate and underprivileged people reside.

Further, in case of the Green Revolution and several other developmental programmes in the first few decades of our Independence, no one can ignore the enormous contribution that radio (All India Radio - AIR) made for making them successful. Keeping up the trend, the last few decades witnessed a huge growth in the medium's scope resulting from significant technological developments.

Over the decades Radio as a medium of communication has played an important role in the nation's socio-cultural, political and economic development. It has the unique advantage of being receivable through low cost, battery operated, and mobile receiving sets, affordable for almost everyone, even in the rural areas. With appropriate strategies, radio can expand its reach to sparsely populated areas and remote corners of the country. In the recent years, Ministry of Information & Broadcasting has initiated a number of steps for the expansion of radio all over the country.

Noted communication expert Daniel Lerner in an in-depth study of the communication dynamics in the middle-eastern nations, found that modernization and economic development is closely involved with urbanization, literacy and mass media. He also found an integrally-close relationship between literacy and exposure to mass media.

They also develop the ability to empathize with others, that is – see themselves in the situation with his or her fellow beings. The person at the same time becomes the cash customer, the Radio listener and the voter accepting and advocating change. So the personality style of modern or civilized man is urbane, literate and participatory. Thus this expert looks upon mass media as a 'mobile multiplier'.

It had secured its position as an amalgam of most of the public institutions and a trusted guest in the homes of millions of people even by the 1930s in the USA. It needs to be mentioned here that the World War II brought the Radio era to a triumphant new high, a much fuller recognition of, and accounting for, Radio's cultural role was at hand. During the 'Great Depression' of the 1930s in the USA, Radio had seized the opportunity of keeping the entire nation informed, entertained and unified through those days of hard economic times and hardships.

The right to communicate and enjoy affordable access to means of mass communication is widely being acknowledged as a fundamental human right nowadays. In fact, the World Association of Community Radio Broadcasters (AMARC) has termed this as a 'universal human right' underpinning all other human rights. It also stresses that this special right needs to be preserved by all means in the face of a rapidly-changing scenario of information and communication technology round the globe. Further, it is worth mentioning that two stalwarts of the media world – Marshal McLuhan and Sean MacBride (MacBride Commission) both have put India into 'Radio Territory'.

Public Service Broadcasting (PSB)

Freedom of speech and expression are generally taken for granted and need not be expressly recognized by law. It is only by imposing restrictions and regulations that the law draws attention to the concept. The extent to which such restrictions and controls are to be found is perhaps a good yardstick to determine how free a society is. A liberal democratic society introduces as few curbs as possible on freedom of speech and expression. And those that have been imposed can and ought to be justified in the larger interests of the society.

Considering all pros and cons of these three systems we can say that a Public Service Broadcaster (PSB) should possess these characteristics --

- It should be a non-governmental public broadcasting. This means that decisions about its tasks, contents, organization, financing should be made publicly, yet should not be made by the existing political (governmental) public institution, but by a separate non-governmental pubic institution. In order to ensure that no ruling establishments do abuse its wide reach for furthering narrow party goals it should be governed only by a politically-independent board or trust. This board should in turn be represented by people from viewers, listeners and others concerned who feel responsible for the political, social and cultural impact of the broadcast programmes. And are also capable of giving appropriate directions to its functioning. These goals should be founded democratically and pluralistically.

- A PSB should be non-commercial public broadcasting. This is because as in general, or at least some specific types of programmes of these bodies have market failures, the decisions about tasks, contents, organization, findings can't be made by market criteria which are suitable and effective for commercial goods only. For the same reasons the benefits of public broadcasters' programmes can't be evaluated by the criteria that are suitable for the evaluation of commercial broadcasting programmes.

Commercial broadcasting on PSB should be restricted for two reasons--

- A PSB should articulate a wide, pluralistic spectrum of issues and views considerably exceeding the range that is relevant from a purely commercial point of view. For example, it should include cultural and religious issues which are of fundamental importance for citizens and for society also. But being non-marketable goods, these issues do not interest commercial broadcasters and not provided by them.
- Commercial broadcasting on PSB involves the risk of commercial and political interests merging and the danger of commercial power being used to steer political power in a non-transparent and anti-democratic way.

It needs to be borne in mind that good quality programmes are a universal support for formal and non-formal education. Quality programmes are always popular. At the same time PSBs have to be accountable to the public and the latter in turn has to accept that PSB is a credible entity even to support education.

"Public service plays an irreplaceable role in providing citizens with information, education and entertainment free from commercial, state or political influence. It must enable each citizen to become a stakeholder in society, participating fully in the life of the community to which they belong and actively involved in its organizations. It must be free from partisan or state pressure. It aims to serve all in the quest for the common good. It must preserve its independence while at the same time having its long-term financial resources guaranteed."

"Neither commercial nor state-controlled, public broadcasting's only raison d'etre is public service. It is the public's broadcasting organization, it speaks to everyone as a citizen. Public broadcasters encourage access to and participation in public life. They develop knowledge, broaden horizons, and enable people to better understand themselves by a better understanding of the world and others," World Radio & Television Council (2002).

Tongue in 1996 argued that democratic societies required shared information or common knowledge in order to function effectively and democratically. She also warns that when differentiation and fragmentation arise within the society, common knowledge is lost. This is a fact which should strengthen the case for public information and PSBs because diversity and access are the key principles of PSB.

She also argued, "PSB has been built on the principle that it is free at the point of use. There is no reason why this principle should be abandoned. The new world of TV with multiple channels and the fragmentation of audiences increases the case for PSB being available to all and by all means via all technologies. This was stated in her report to the EU's Committee on Culture, Youth, Education and the Media.

The PSBs must be used regularly by the citizens as a prerequisite for living up to their cultural, social and political obligations. On the other hand they have to do so by serving the audiences with a range of contents and services not found in the general media market. These two sets of more or less conflicting requirements are analyzed and discussed leading to a tentative answer to the central question – is public broadcasting by its contents offer making a difference or has it by the forces of market competition been tempted or forced to join the mainstream.

It is common knowledge that there is a unique nature and importance of personal as well as mass communication for individuals and society. This not only justifies but also requires public 'interference' with the media to prevent them serving only particularistic and lucrative interests. Whereas the general idea of public service points out the principles of equal access to consumption of important services or goods without any reference to the need of publicness in particular, the case of public service media is different.

Media are the guardians of the principle of publicness in modern democracies, which is central to the concept of public service media. Communicative action of citizens is one of the most important virtues of democracy, because it enables citizens to participate in public deliberations and decision making. Without an effective power of civil society to influence public service media in terms of values, interests and preferences, the idea of public service media would be deprived of its constitutive principles of publicness.

In some cases, as the potential for broadcasting to be used for manipulating public opinion was properly recognized, financing through licence fees was seen in many nations as a means for diminishing the potential for government interference with content if funding came from tax receipts. As a result, licence fees are seen as having these distinct advantages –

First, it assigns the cost for broadcasting directly to the consumers.

Secondly, this tends to create a mutual and reciprocal sense of responsibility between the broadcasters and the audiences, which in turn frees the broadcasters from control and influence by governments (as might be the case where direct government support exists) or advertisers (as might be the case in commercial systems).

Across Europe, currently there is a broad political consensus that every country should have a PSB. The Amsterdam Protocol adopted in 1998 by the Council of Ministers of the European Union (EU) recognized that "the system of public broadcasting in the member states is directly related to the democratic, social and cultural needs of each society and to the need to preserve media pluralism".

A PSB can be defined above all by its remit, which generally includes information, culture, education, the organization of pluralism, promotion of minority cultures etc. In several countries, it has been recognized that PSB has a major role to play in the development of digital terrestrial TV.

The UNESCO definition of a PSB is somewhat like this — "PSB is broadcasting made for the public and financed and controlled by the public. It is neither commercial nor state-owned. It is free from political interference and pressure from commercial forces. Through PSB, citizens are informed, educated and also entertained. When guaranteed with pluralism, programming diversity, editorial independence, appropriate funding, accountability and transparency, PSB can serve as a cornerstone of democracy."

The Indian Context

In this regard two important developments can be cited.

First, the Task Force on Information and Broadcasting set up for the Xth Five-Year Plan recommended that CRs should be run as PSBs. The operational model to be followed is somewhat on the lines of a similar one prevalent in the USA. The idea being that donations and grants etc. can make them keep afloat without coming under undue pressure from any quarter including the government or large corporate houses or media groups for programme contents.

Secondly, in a bid to do away with at least some amount of state control over the medium and also to expand it for public welfare, the MIB introduced the concept of private FM stations and Community Radio stations in the decade of the 1990s. Today, there are about 200 operational CRs in the country along with an MIB plan for expanding the FM network of the country to about a thousand spread over a period of time in the near and distant future.

Besides, another important development in the Indian media scenario has been the initiative for utilizing Radio's huge potential for furthering the educational perspective which is just waiting to be tapped, catering to specific target groups based on sex, age and vocation in the days to come.

In fact, Indian Radio has about a five-decade old rich legacy of working towards educational purposes. Major projects in this direction include Rural Radio Forums for agricultural development (1967), promotion of adult literacy rate, GRAMSAT experiment of 1995 using the medium for training women *panchayat* members etc. These experiments have yielded valuable lessons on software, hardware, organizational management etc. to the organization. In this direction another significant development has been strongly making its presence felt since the last few years.

Media critic and veteran journalist Amit Desai in a book strongly opines that the key attention requirement for the country is to go for 'local broadcasting', reflecting issues of concern for the community. He also stressed upon advocacy for and provision for training NGOs and communities for using the medium towards such a goal as a few of them are practicing at present in different parts of the country.

A pioneer in this field is the Indira Gandhi National Open University (IGNOU) dedicated towards spreading education in the far and wide corners of the country and abroad through the distance education mode. It was in December 2001 that it started setting up a series of FM Radio stations at a few selected places under an ambitious scheme called Gyan Vani which is gradually being expanded all over the country with a mandate to increase it to a hundred. These centres have a coverage capacity of about 60-70 kilometre radius each, sufficient enough for a better broadcasting service aimed at educational purposes. The signals can be further transferred by relay system to long distances by using the existing network of transmitters of AIR.

Radio being the most common and easily-affordable as well as convenient vehicle of mass communication this utilization is only a fraction of the total potential of the medium. Though remaining in hybernation for quite sometime almost all over the world it has already revived itself with ever newer formats and programme varieties.

This initiative brings into fore an interesting development. That is, at least in our country Radio has primarily been associated with the entertainment aspect since the time we became familiar with it. A major contributor to this mindset is that prior to the recent initiative, no significant effort was adopted ever for utilizing the educational aspect of the medium.

Of course, there were some amount of Radio airtime devoted to programmes based on formal educational curriculums, yet they were far from enough to cater to such a large target audience. It is only now that an overwhelming effort has been taken up in this direction. This ambitious step is poised to take the concept of 'electronic learning' process or simply 'e-learning' method to ever greater heights in the days to come.

The moot question here is what is the justification of this glowing discrimination between the two media. All these negative developments are gradually and steadily leading to a major erosion of listenership of this highly-effective medium for development. Along with the declining popularity of this medium – an important potential for disseminating information for development purposes – it is also registering a rapid downfall in the overall analysis. This is what is being reflected in the latest trends of ownership and audiences of this medium of the masses.

The India Census 2011 has reflected an important and alarming development. That is, the percentage of households owning at least one radio receiver set all over the nation has gone down from an impressive 35.1% in 2001 to 19.9% in 2011 Census. This is quite a steep fall just within a matter of one single decade. This is in light of the intense competition among various media for cornering more and more percentage of the audience base. The drop is more alarming at 20% for urban areas from 44.5% to 25.3 while in rural areas it is about 15% from 31.5 (2001) to 17.3 (2011). (India Census, 2011 – Table No I, II, III). As the table here reflects adequately, this negative growth is more in rural areas of the country than in urban areas.

First of all, AIR has not yet been able to shed its long-lasting image as simply being a government spokesperson as a whole for all its programmes. Initially it was established with the objective of developing it as a PSB modelled under the British Broadcasting Corporation (BBC). But, down the decades of its existence till now, this organization has lost its true glory either way. It has failed to prove its worth as a PSB and continuing to function only as an information-dissemination agency of the union government. This is a sheer wastage of opportunities as AIR has a reach and coverage of more than 99% of the population and also geographical areas of the country.

Secondly, the MIB as discussed above, has never allowed any competition to grow for AIR and even development of a proper PSB system independent of AIR.

There is yet another negative development for this particular medium. The recent CNN-IBN-*The Hindu* Election Tracker Survey, conducted by the Centre for the Study of Developing Societies (CSDS), Delhi found that only 12% of Indian voters actually accessed radio for news whereas the same for TV stands at a high of 42%. (*The Hindu*, 2013). This study was conducted with 20,000 respondents across 267 constituencies in 18 states of the country.

Table 1: Media Exposure

How Regularly do You do the Following for News ?

	Daily	*Sometimes*	*Barely*	*Never*	*No Opinion*
Watch TV	42	26	11	17	4
Read newspaper	29	19	10	34	8
Listen to the radio	12	22	14	44	8
Use the internet /go online	5	7	6	66	16

Source: The Hindu, July 29, 2013, page 3

In the Indian context, there has been numerous calls for democratizing the information-dissemination system. It is expected to encourage an optimum level of participation of the target audiences in the programme-making process and thereby determine their own development agenda. However, things have not proved successful in that sense yet. In this regard, the situation in the African continent and also in case of our neighbour Nepal are highly encouraging.

Youths Continue to be Primary Listeners

Indian Readership Survey (IRS) is one of the largest readership surveys conducted in the country. It also captures listenership for radio. According to IRS 2012 Q3 findings, the listenership of radio increased from 155 million to 159 million from Q1 2012 to Q3 2012 registering a growth of 6.1% compared to 6.4 percent growth of Television during the same period.

Significantly, majority of radio listenership comes from the age group of 20-40 years. As a result stations continue to focus on youth by developing youth-centric programming. (FICCI, 2013)

Age Group	*% Listener Ship*
Below 20 years	27%
20 - 40 years	48%
Above 40 years	26%

Source: FICCI, 2013

There was an announcement by the then Finance Minister of India in the 2013 budget about the rollout of 839 stations across 294 cities is an encouraging development for this medium.

Conclusion

It is found that in spite of all roadblocks in front of this immensely-potential medium, it has always been able to fight back to regain its lost territory. As the medium never relented in its struggle for growth and development, it can be very well expected that in the coming future also it is going to be on a steady trajectory tackling all its hindrances head on. That is highly necessary from the point of view of dissemination of information to the masses at the grassroots level and thereby educating the people in the long run. It would be definitely a good idea to promote and encourage this medium with all our efforts involving all the stakeholders - civil society, government, private players all. The future of the medium is quite bright enough though its proper utilization would depend upon how much we are able to take advantage of its multi-faceted positive aspects.

REFERENCES

Aitchison, Jim, *Cutting edge Radio – how to create the world's best radio ads for brands in the 21st century*, Prentice Hall, 2002,

AIR website,

Barua UL, This is All India Radio, April, 1983, Publication Division, Ministry of Information & Broadcasting, Government of India),

Folkerts, Jean & Lacy, Stephen, *The Media in your life – an introduction to mass communication*, First India reprint 2005, Pearson Education (Singapore) Pvt Ltd,

Hilmes, Michele &Loviglio, Jason, *Radio Reader – essays in the cultural history of radio,*Rouledge, London/New York), India Census 2001,

Mass Communication in India – JV Vilanilam,

Ministry of Information & Broadcasting (MIB) Annual Report 2004 - 05),

National Readership Survey (NRS 2005),

Pavarala, Vinod & Kumar, Kanchan, *Enabling Community Radio: Case studies in national broadcasting policy,* MICA Communications Review, Vol. 1, No 3, 2004, MICA, Ahmedabad,

Press Council of India Collection of articles – 2005,

Padmanabhan, BS, *Dedicated to the public good,* Frontline, September 23, 2005,

Padmanabhan, BS, *Modernizing and moving ahead,* (interview with Mr KS Sharma, former Chief Executive officer of Prasar Bharati), Frontline, October 7, 2005,

Reddy, Jaipal (former Union I & B Minister), Cabinet nod for big boost to FM radios, *The Hindu* front page, July 1, 2005,

Srivastava, KM, Importance of mother tongue – radio programming for rural women and children, Media Mind – III, Occasional Papers, IIMC, Dhenkanal, September 2003,

Singhal, Arvind & Rogers, M Everett, India's communication revolution – from bullock carts to cyber marts, Sage Publication, New Delhi, First India reprint 2001,

The Hindu, September 21, 2007 (page 10),

9

Radio as a Medium for Storytelling

Radhika Chugh

Nina Sabnani (2009) describes storytelling as the 'memories or mediation between reality and aspirations that reflects what a society wishes to express about itself. It has a way of mesmerizing the listeners into silence and the tellers into expressing the deepest desires and anxieties of their society, directly or through subversive means.' Storytelling has been an important aspect of the rich oral tradition of India and stories are passed on as collective cultural wisdom to each subsequent generation.They can be read as sociological artefacts which house within them the cultural memory of a society. Considering the importance of oral narratives as a reflection of the society and culture, it is necessary to take a look at the modern forms of storytelling.

Some easily identifiable attributes of radio include the fast pace of message transmission, lack of geographical limits

Radhika has pursued Bachelors in Journalism from Lady Shri Ram College for Women and is presently working as a Sub-Editor at Inshorts Media Labs. She enjoys keeping up with the current happenings around the world, and believes that communication is the building block at the core of every human undertaking, regardless of its orientation.

binding it, transient nature of its content and the inexpensive and unencumbered technology associated with it. Since this paper discussed radio as a medium of storytelling, the following section expands on the characteristics that aid the practice of storytelling through radio.

Radio is often held as a blind medium, propelled by the listeners' imagination. While a picture is indisputably worth a thousand words, sounds alone can be manipulated to create a wide spectrum of impressions on the listener without incurring the heavy cost of acquiring lavish sets. Even though the medium is blind, it is visually evocative to the extent that it assists the creation of congruent mental images in the listeners' mind.

When propped in comparison with to other mass mediums, radio has the capacity to percolate to the deepest trenches of human civilization. But this ability doesn't discount it from being a deeply individual medium. While watching television is a collective exercise, listening to radio is often a personal experience that transports the listener to the plane created by the radio presenters. In addition to being a private medium, radio also works as background score in the sense that it does not demand the undivided attention of its listeners. The radio often assumes the background as the listener goes about his day. This makes the medium deeply pervasive in the everyday activities of its listeners. However, in order for radio content to capture the listeners' attention and make a lasting impact, the presenter has to employ aurally evocative cues such that his/her show does not get lost in the background.

Importance of Oral Traditions

Oral traditions constitute the intangible cultural heritage of a society. Professional storytellers, poets and performers pass on the collective wisdom of the community through their art, through reproduction, improvisation and new creative expression infused with age old tales.

In its discussion about the role of oral traditions in a society, the Milwaukee Public Museum explains,

"Oral tradition is important in all societies, despite the reliance of some cultures on written records and accounts. These traditions account for the ways things are and often the way they should be, and assist people in educating the young and teaching important lessons about the past and about life. While oral traditions can vary from teller to teller, variations are also open to contradiction in the same ways that written accounts are. The force of oral tradition can continue through generations although small details in the telling may change.

India has seen a culture of oral traditions persist through generations. Some refined form of storytelling which form an integral unit of oral narratives include *Burrakatha of Andhra Pradesh, Pandavani of Chattisgarh, Garodas of Gujarat etc.* These oral narratives are performed by a narrator in front of audiences, where different techniques of storytelling such as singing and enacting, are employed to keep the listener engaged. Recurrent themes in the narrative include universal emotions such as love, heroism and chivalry, which are bound to resonate with the listener.

An insight into the oral traditions of a culture reveals a vast body of knowledge pertaining to the kinships, customs, traditions and relationships within a community. It provides insights into the cultural practices, perceptions about gender roles and even leisure activities. The need to preserve oral traditions has never been more urgent. According to a research conducted by the National Geographic, more than half of the 7,000 plus languages spoken on Earth may disappear in the time to come, taking away with them the traces of heritage and culture that they bloomed in.

Oral traditions thrive on intertextuality, and freely borrow from the literature popular in the collective memory of the community. Faroqui M. writes (2010), "In the process of telling the story, narrators freely borrowed tropes and themes from other stories, thus it was that Rumi Masnavi and Arabian

Nights both came to contain many stories from the Panchtantra tradition." Similarly, the *mandali* members in radio telling, who have grown up in an environment of storytelling, borrow identifiable topes and themes from other literature while retaining the originality of their own creation. For example, the radio story *Aur Bol Pada Hiraan* by Akbar Quadri references folklore within the narrative, leading through to a seamless flow.

Radio storytelling has been responsible for the reworking of oral traditions in India. While oral traditions aré usually community practice of collective listening, storytelling through radio allows the listeners to achieve a heightened sense of intimacy with the narrator because listening to the radio is an increasingly individual activity. The para social relationship that the listener shares with the narrator deepens since the listener often gets mystified by the medium in a way that he/ she remains unaware about the rest of the audience tuning in for the show. (Wolfenden, 2012)

Radio and Storytelling

Radio presents various advantages as a medium for storytelling, the foremost being its ability to create images in the listeners mind through the use of sound. The same story is well disposed to create varying impacts on different listeners, depending upon their ability to receive aural cues and picture the narrative playing out. It's also possible for the story to move relatively quickly, in terms of locations and settings, which is often used to the advantage of the plot. This allows for variety and contrast in the stories, since setting of the plot can be anything from the realm of human imagination.

Storytelling for radio is different from storytelling for other mediums because the listener does not have the luxury to revisit parts of the story. The sentence structure has to be clear and concise, such that the listener understands the narrative in the first go. Long, convoluted and complex sentences can prove to be counterproductive for the plot. There is no scope of ambiguity in the sentence structure, lest the flow of the narrative is broken and the spell of storytelling shattered. The choice of words is also critical for the listeners' comprehension of the drama. Storytellers are cautious with the use of homophones since they can be sources of ambiguity, causing incongruity in the narrative for the listener. In crafting such narratives for radio, storytellers often discard the 'mass medium' approach and address the audience in first person to establish an intimate connection between the narrator and the listener. (McLeish, 2005)

The prime duty of a writer is to employ the techniques of drama to create comprehensive images in the listener's mind and fuel his/her imagination. The medium of radio pushes listeners to create unique mental images based on the information provided in the storyteller. The amount of information supplied should be treated as an act of balance. If the narrative is dotted with too much information, the listener may get overwhelmed and find it hard to keep up with the flow of the story. On the contrary, if the information supplied by the storyteller is insufficient, the listener may feel disoriented.

Tim Burton has famously said that every story should have a beginning, middle and end but not necessarily in the same order. Radio drama follows the basic narrative structure of explaining the situation, introducing the conflict, developing action and resolving the conflict. However, there is no compulsion on the writer to abide by this chronology. He/She is encouraged to play to the advantages of the radio medium and add intriguing complications, mysteries, plot twists and sub plots in order to produce engaging content. Storytelling on radio often takes parabolic routes in order to keep the audience listening in rapt attention. The key features of the dominant form of narrative structure, as enumerated by Anders Hasen (1993) include

- A single diegesis: there is one main storyline.
- A central pattern of enigma and resolution is followed.
- All questions posed at the start of the narrative, or as it progresses, are answered.

- The chain of events follow a logical sequence, and has an inner logic.
- Verisimilitude: all events are believable.
- The audience should empathise with the central characters.
- The focus of the narrative is on individuals rather than society or groups.
- Technical and symbolic elements are subordinate to the construction of the narrative and the need to drive it along.

Since radio is concerned with creation of images with words alone, the mood and colour of the plot are based on the use of aurally evocative cues words and sounds. The acoustics are manipulated to create different ambiences. In monophonic perspective, the move from a busy street to a reverberant courtroom can be denoted by a modification in the acoustic environment. (Robert Mcleish 2005)

The ambient sounds that play through a scene can be seen as an equivalent of a theatre's backdrop. The incidental furniture in the backdrop of a visual performance, such as a dining table, a telephone or wine glasses can be replaced by sounds such as the creaking of a chair, ringing of the telephone and the sound of wine being poured in a glass in the case of radio drama. These diegetic sounds help to establish the scene and furnish the mental images created by the listener. In the everyday routine of life, one encounters a medley of complex sounds. However, in storytelling in radio, the sound producer infuses sounds which are not just real, but also understandable and convincing. Sounds can also be seen as socially shared codes and conventions, which add layers of meaning to the narrative. The sound of a clock ticking usually connotes a prolonged passage of time, an owl hooting can connote an eerie night and sound of footsteps is often used to heighten the drama.

While the importance of sound effects cannot be undermines, music plays just as critical role as an indispensable component of storytelling on radio, and is an ally for to the resourceful writer. When used in inordinate amounts, it can distract the listener. However, when used innovatively, music can tie the entire plot together via the agency of leitmotif and can create the right moods for the plot.

It is necessary to understand that radio isn't the medium for wreathing and narrating complex stories with an overwhelming number of sub plots. Radio is a background medium which allows its audience to go on with their tasks of the day as the radio plays on, since it doesn't demand their full attention.

Radio Audiences and Presenters

Radio audiences are not just financial assets for broadcasting firms, but also a site of cultural enquiry for academicians. The relationship between radio presenters and their audiences is not as plain sailing as it may seem on the surface. The para-social interaction where the audience experiences close affinity with the presenter, is a carefully constructed phenomenon. Horton and Wohl (1956), in their study of para-social interaction have coined the term 'persona' to describe the person who creates such pervasive bonds with an unidentified mass of the audience. Throwing light on the calculative nature of the construction of persona, they write, "The persona may be considered by his audience as a friend, counsellor, comforter, and model; but, unlike real associates, he has the peculiar virtue of being standardized according to the 'formula' for his character and performance which he and his managers have worked out and embodied in an appropriate 'production format'."(Horton & Wohl, 1956, p.217)

The workspace for radio presenters is set in social isolation, where there is no instant way to gauge the immediate impact created on the audience. The composition of the audience tuning in is unknown to the presenter, who has to create social contexts which have a universal appeal.

Media theorists such as Ien Ang and Paddy Scannell have refuted the possibilities of being able to wholly know one's audience composition. They have discredited audience ratings by maintaining that audience research has been institutionalized to milk commercial gains, by pitting them to sponsors and advertisers. Quantitative data cannot do justice in representing the audience, which then remains unknown, invisible and unidentified. However, the operationalization of audiences to include target markets and target audiences and create 'industry knowledge' has become the norm in the broadcast industry. Despite this straight jacketed conception of audience, presenters strive to look beyond the numbers and demographics and manage emotional bonds with them.

Even though Yaadon ka Idiot Box is in a format of its own kind, the Indian radio has seen the presence of some very prominent radio personalities. Any recounting about the Indian radio and leisure would be incomplete without the mention of the legendary show popular by the name Binaca Geetmala. It was a weekly radio countdown show of top songs from Hindi cinema listened to by millions of Hindi music lovers. It ran from 1953 to 1994. It was partly because of the presenter Ameen Sayani that the show was able to receive create the inordinate amount of fandom in the Indian audiences. The show was responsible for giving shape to the Mumbai filmmaker's imagination of a national audience (Punathambekar article: Ameen Sayani and Radio Ceylon 2010)

REFERENCES

Farooqui, M. (2010). Retrieved 9th March 2017, from http://dastangoi.blogspot.in/p/dastangoi-lost-art-form-of-urdu.html

Hasen, A. (1993) *Qualitative Research Methods.* SAGE Publications, Inc; 1 edition.

Horton D. and Wohl R. *Mass Communication and Para-social Interaction: Observations on Intimacy at a Distance'*, Psychiatry 19: 215-29

McLeish, R. (2005) *Radio Production (Fifth Edition).* Focal Press.

Milwaukee Public Museum. Retrieved 9th March 2017, from https://www.mpm.edu/wirp/ICW-14.html

National Geographic. Retrieved 9th March 2017, from http://travel.nationalgeographic.co.in/travel/enduringvoices/.

Sabnani, N. (2009). The kaavad storytelling tradition of Rajasthan. *Design Thoughts,* (2), 28-33. Retrieved 9th March 2017, from http://www.idc.iitb.ac.in/resources/dt-july-2009/kaavad.pdf

Wolfenden, H, (2012). I know exactly who they are': radio presenters' conceptions of audience. *Radio Evolution: Conference Proceeding September, 14-16, 2011, Braga, University of Minho: Communication and Society Research Centre.* Retrieved 9th March, 2017, from http://www.lasics.uminho.pt/ojs../index.php/radioevolution/article/view/857/810

10

'Mann ki Baat' Used for Development Communication

Parnika Deorais

There are a wide range of interpretations for the theme of development communication, but it generally means communication that can be used for development. It is about using communication to change or improve something. It is important to understand first what communication means in this context. "Communication" can be considered a comprehensive term, encompassing all forms of human interactions, from the interpersonal to the mediated ones, and from the one-way linear flow to the two way dialogic processes (Mefalopulos, 2008).

Development communication has to deal with two types of audience: (i) the communicators comprising development bureaucracy, media practitioners and professionals, and (ii) the people i.e. the audience that can be informed or uninformed; educated or semi literate or literate (Kumar 2011). Main features of development communication – Social

Parnika Deora is a Journalism graduate from Lady Shri Ram College for Women, University of Delhi. She is currently pursuing her Masters in Public Policy from St. Xaviers, Mumbai and is a keen follower of national as well as international political events.

Transformation, communicators and audiences, reach and its two way communication process.

To understand this phenomenon better we need to understand the three models designed after development communication soon after the World war two-

1. The Modernization Paradigm

This paradigm came into being after the World War II, where 'underdeveloped' countries were to be bought out of their miseries of poverty and stagnation by modernizing their economic process and introducing free market approaches.

Diffusion and Innovations theory would be used here to make those countries adapt to the values and ideas to achieve the goals. During the Cold war, the effect of the influence of both the super powers could be seen in almost all aspects of global world order and that is why the modernization paradigm promoted by political scientists and scholars of Western countries became so strong and so pervasive in every dimension of social life that it became also known as the "dominant paradigm" (Mefalopulos, 2008).

At the technological level it meant faith in the scientific method. At the cultural level this paradigm meant abandoning traditional beliefs and moving forward with attitudes important for modernizing. Economically it meant understanding the power of free markets and on the political level it required the adoption of democratic systems (Mefalopulos, 2008).

Critics of this paradigm attacked its predominant, if not exclusive, economic focus. In its quest to develop, modernization neglected to consider the relevance of other social dimensions and failed to take into account a number of historical and broader socio political factors (Servaes 1991) that impeded the autonomous development of many developing countries. Also it is a one way communication process where the developed nations are influencing their ideology and will on the underdeveloped or developing nations.

2. Dependency and World Systems Theory

This theory which originated in 1970s in Latin America states that the world is comprised of two parts - core (the rich countries) and periphery (the poor countries). The imbalances in the world were mainly due to past patters of domination and division of labour. The core countries use their technological superiority and know-how and economic power to strengthen their lead while the periphery countries end up supplying raw materials and cheap labour to the rich countries. By ascribing causes of underdevelopment exclusively to the centres of international capitalism, dependency theorists failed to consider relevant internal causes contributing to the problem (Mefalopulos, 2008), such as the role played by national elites.

Immanuel Wallerstein in the 1970s conceptualised the world systems theory where he addressed the criticism that it was very convenient to divide the world into two parts. So he came up with the core (rich countries), periphery (poor countries) and semi periphery (higher levels of resources than the majority of developing countries). He says that all the causes for development and underdevelopment can be considered internal to the capitalist system, on the basis of the international division of labour and the control of raw resources.

The proponents of the dependency theory vigorously supported a more balanced flow of communication at the international level. Yet, at the national level, they often neglected to consider the horizontal component of communication within countries and failed to give proper attention to the potential of privately owned media and community media, focusing through the state's perspective (Mefalopulos, 2008).

3. The Emerging Participatory Paradigm

Participation is important for development, because it leads to a shift from seeing people as passive recipients to being active agents. Common features of this perspective are the emphasis on people, the endogenous vision of development, and the attention to power, rights and issues. White (1982) summarized the following factors for the increased rate of adoption in participatory development processes–

- services are provided at lower costs
- participation has intrinsic values for participants
- participation is a catalyst for further development efforts
- participation leads to a sense of responsibility for the project
- participation ensures the use of indigenous knowledge and expertise

In this paradigm there is a two way communication flow and the top down features rooted in the modernization paradigm get diluted, facilitating empowerment and participation. Example of participatory approaches:

PRA (participatory rural appraisal): It started to become popular in the 1980s as a research method trying to reach a balance between researchers' needs to be scientific in their approach and the communities' rights to participate in activities concerning their own well-being. By spending extended periods of time in the community, PRA researchers were expected to better understand and pay closer attention to the needs and problems identified and defined by the community (Mefalopulos, 2008).

Development Communication in India

During the first development decade the stress was on national development through social growth. The models of community development and Panchayati Raj were essential in participatory communication. At that time most of the international development community were adopting the Dominant Paradigm. In the second development decade, India switched over to the Dominant Paradigm and the stress was on modernization through industrialization. In the 1970s and also currently, the two development models of participatory communication and basic needs models, after which came the New Paradigm of Development, is on the rise (Kumar, 2011).

India's earliest organized experiments in development communication were held in the 1960s, sponsored by India's universities and other educational institutions, and by the Bretton Woods school institutions. In the coming times, development communication in India played two roles–The first is a transformational role through which it seeks social change in the direction of higher quality of life and social justice. The second is a socialization role through which it strives to maintain some of the established values of society that are consonant with development (Kaul, 2011).

In the Indian context we shall focus on two things that are important in this aspect of development communication–

- democratic decentralization
- narrowcasting

Democratic Decentralization–Initially there was a top down approach that was prevalent in the country when it came to communication development goals to the masses. Priorities and goals were set in Delhi and communicated to people of the lower strata and people were not actively involved in the grassroot level. Gradually came the practice of democratic decentralization where the people at the grassroot level were also involved in the decision-making process. A group of people residing at a specific place are the best people to know what they want for development along with how they want the developmental plans to be executed, on what priority etc. This is the reason for which the concept of 'local-self governments' was conceived and implemented (Kaul, 2011).

Narrowcasting–To disseminate information in the form of electronic waves to the maximum number of people possible is called Broadcasting. So in the early says of mass communication, broadcasting was used to send across information to the masses. The problem here was that this information was general in nature and had no community specifications. Narrowcasting' is the opposite of this concept. Here, mass media is split up into viable smaller units so that it can be brought closer to the masses to the best possible extent, best example being community radio.

Mann ki Baat

'Mann Ki Baat' is an Indian radio programme hosted by Prime Minister Narendra Modi in which he addresses the people of the nation on radio, DD National and DD News. It is also broadcast by some private news channels as and when it happens. This program is run by the All India Radio and it started on 3rd October 2014. Till now 15 episodes have been broadcast with the recent one being on 26 February 2017.

This show is one of its kinds that PM Narendra Modi initiated with the aim of reaching out to the masses and using his popularity and the reach of the radio to talk about development issues and policies. Some important features of the Mann ki Baat program are-

- The program is always in Hindi language which is easy to understand and caters to a vast section to the society who is not well read in English.
- The program always focuses on the issue currently in news and is used by the PM to create awareness about policies, laws, issues, etc.
- It reaches more than 90% of the population through the radio and that is why its penetration and audience involvement is commendable.
- This program is repeated at 8pm on the same day of the broadcast, in different regional languages so that it could be understood by one and all.
- It also has a feature in which people can listen to 'Mann ki Baat' by calling on a specific number through their phones.

An Overview of the Program

The program was started on the auspicious day of Vijaya Dashmi on 30th October, 2014. Through Akashvani, Prime Minister Narendra Modi tries to reach the vast population especially in the rural areas. AIR reaches 90% of the population and that is one of the major reasons why it was chosen for the broadcast of this program.

Also, this show has led to the revival of AIR. Over the years the popularity of Akahsvani saw a dip with the coming of television and then the internet. Their listeners had dropped with response to news and special programes but 'Mann ki Baat' was a fresh new thrust. The revenue of AIR has also increased after it started broadcasting this show.

A very important feature of development communication is its paradigms that have been discussed earlier. Keeping in mind the new development paradigm and the new communication approach, the following things are required in the process of development communication (Kaul, 2011)-

1. Equality of the distribution of social and economic benefits, information and education.
2. Popular participation in development planning and execution, accompanied by decentralization of activities to the local level.
3. Self-reliance and independence in development with emphasis on the potential of local resources.
4. Integration of traditional with modern systems, so that development is a syncretisation of old and new ideas, with the exact mixture somewhat different in each locale.

'Mann ki Baat' is a program that tries and to an extent is able to reach some goals of development communication. The following points will be make this easier to understand-

- PM Modi has used this program to talk and motivate people to take part in development campaigns like, 'Swachh Bharat Abhiyan', 'Beti Bachao, Beti Padhao',

'Amrut Scheme', 'Start up India, Stand up India', 'Digital India' and many more. He made sure that through radio he is able to tell the masses about the campaigns and get them to work on them too. For example–After talking about cleanliness and its importance, the government got responses from people all over the country as to how they were (on an individual and community level) working on it.

- This platform is extensively used by the government to talk about its policies and schemes like–'Acquisition of Land Bill', 'Sovereign Gold Bonds', 'Amrut Scheme', 'Direct Benefit Transfer Scheme', 'Lucky Grahak Yojana', 'Digi Dhan VyapaarYojana' etc. The radio programme is already creating impact. It's good to learn that over 10 million well-to-do families voluntarily gave up LPG gas subsidy for the benefit of disadvantaged population lacking access to clean cooking fuel (Ahuja, 2016).
- The program has led to increased sales for Khadi products (125% increase) as Modi focused on growth of indigenous products and the fact that the sales of Khadi increased, shows that this source of communication helps in yielding results.
- A very important feature of development communication is a two way communication/ information flow. This is extensively focused on through 'Mann ki Baat'. Use of social media like Twitter, Facebook, government website, comments, mail etc. has been commendable. For example- (a) for tackling and spreading awareness about the drug menace in Punjab, the government came with "Drugs Free India", (b) for promoting tourism there was "Incredible India" and "Yes We Can" for elimination of poverty, giving quality healthcare to all, end of terrorism, jobs for all, global peace etc.
- Apart from just social media, the government allows people to give feedback on their website

'www.mygov.in' and also allows them to download and make use of the App–'NarendraModiApp' for necessary communication and information.

- Digital divide is a rampant problem in our country and because the rural population is specifically targeted through 'Mann ki Baat', it is highly important that they are able to provide necessary feedback. These people may not have access to social media and Internet so for them the government has allowed posting feedbacks to Akashvani's office where they are vetted and then broadcast.

For example–To reach the people at the grassroot level who might not have access to new media technologies; the government has given them an address to post their letters and feedbacks. Through these programs the government increases awareness about a number of health, environmental, sanitation and other issues. For example, on Tuberculosis Day the people were made aware about the disease and how to prevent it. They were also informed that there are 4 lakh free DOT providers and that those are a must.

- *Foreign Policy*: The PM makes sure that through this medium, the people in the most remote of the country can be up to date regarding the country's international standing and foreign policy developments. When Ex American President, Mr. Barack Obama visited India, a special Mann ki Baat was organised where Mr. Obama was seen answering questions that were sent by the people of the country. Whether it's about the PM's foreign trips or any huge deal signed with any other country, it is mentioned through this program.
- This programme is also an incredibly powerful initiative that has enabled Mr. Modi to create an emotional bond and win the minds and hearts of millions of people across the country. Through this initiative, he informs, educates, inspires, shares, reminds and urges the people about everything that can contribute to nation-building. (Ahuja, 2016). The

program many times focuses on the contributions of the common people who have worked for the development of the country. Also many times the PM talks about our brave soldiers are keeping us safe and who deserve to be respected and applauded for their work.

- Mr. Modi makes sure that people feel included and a part of the show, which is why he often reads out letters and feedbacks sent to him by the common people. He also praises initiatives and changes that individuals have brought about in respect to development or any other social issue. Example–The program broadcast on 25th December 2015 included the work done by Dileep Singh Malviya who built 100 toilets in Bhojpura village for the people there. His efforts were applauded by the PM.
- This program has also led to revival of Radio.

AIR

Radio broadcasting has been one of the contributors to the national development for around six decades through All India Radio (AIR), officially known since 1956 as Akashvani (Voice from the Sky), which is the national public radio broadcaster of India and a division of Prasar Bharati. However, the advent of television providing audio-visual format and later social networking has affected the medium.

With a reach of about 99% of the country's population, this programme through Aakashvani creates a direct connect with every corner of the country. Under PM Modi, All India Radio is proving to be an affable tool in disseminating fundamental social messages and articulating the challenges and infinite possibilites of development through communication.

Using radio for development communication has been in practice since 1940s. Tracing its history we have to go back to communities who listened to rural radio broadcasts in the 1940s. One distinguishing element of those early programs was that they focused on the use of indigenous languages–Marathi,

Gujarati and Kannada. India's earliest organized experiments in development communication were held in the 1960s, sponsored by India's universities and other educational institutions. (Kaul, 2011)

There are three common types of development campaigns: Persuasion, changing what people do; Education, changing social values; and Informing, empowering people to change by increasing knowledge (Kaul,2011).

'Mann ki Baat' is a Mix of Development Communication Models

Before we discuss the two models that come together to get best results for this program, we need to discuss about 'development threshold'. This underlies that communication efforts should be tailored to the needs, psychological dispositions of people and the development threshold of people. It's not news that there is a stark difference between the development threshold of urban and rural society. This difference is called the 'development gap' which is prominent in a country like India. Development gap suggests that people in different development thresholds need different development communication handling for effective development (Kumar, 2011).

The unique thing about 'Mann ki Baat' is that it tries to lessen the development gap by accommodating the development thresholds of both, the urban and the rural society. For example–the radio programme is already creating impact. It's good to learn that over 10 million well-to-do families voluntarily gave up LPG gas subsidy for the benefit of disadvantaged population lacking access to clean cooking fuel. The fact that the program could link the success of a scheme to the efforts of the urban people in aiding the rural people is a great step forward.

While discussing development communication it is important to understand that the communication media are, in the context of development, generally used to support development initiatives by the dissemination of messages that encourage the public to support development-oriented projects (Servaes, 2008). The hierarchical view on communication can be summarized in two ways and 'Mann ki Baat' has taken up important features from both these models–

(a) Diffusion of Innovations

The main focus of this approach is the adoption of technological and social innovations through diffusion of new ideas, services and products. Diffusion of both material and social innovations is necessary. Individual and community decisions for acceptance and rejection of innovations depend primarily on the needs of the adopters. What is communicated about the innovations and how it is communicated are very important for development (Kumar, 2011).

The fact that Radio is extensively being used for this communication is a good example of this model. To be able to listen to the program, people have started adopting new ways and using new technologies. Radio has seen its revival but apart from that, the usage of internet to listen to 'Mann ki Baat' has led to a new innovation where people can log onto 'mygov.in' site and listen to all the past programs. They can also call on a certain number and listen to PM Modi talk. Such new practices have been given a boost by making it so easily available to the people. This diffusion of new practices and uses of technology has been a major outcome of this program. He uses these platforms to tell people about new applications and technology through which they can move towards a 'Digital India'.

Here diffusion allows people to move from a traditional way of life to take up new innovations that allows them to set in a more developed and technologically advanced way of life. The American scholar Everett Rogers is said to be the person who introduced this diffusion theory in the context of development. Here, mass media plays an important role in spreading information and awareness about new practices and innovations but it was seen that the stage where one has to decide whether or not he/she will adopt that new innovation depends largely on personal communication. Therefore, the general conclusion of this line of thought is that mass communication is less likely than personal influence to have a direct effect on social behaviour.

But the catch here is that the government has tried to make this program as personal as possible. The program format is such that it seems like a conversation between the general public and the Prime Minister of the country. He voices the opinions and feedbacks of the masses and in return talks to them about different schemes and policies. This personalization of the program has actually helped in people adopting and inculcating certain practices that the Prime Minister talks about.

Diffusion on innovations is a top down vertical form of communication. When the program is going on then at that time only the Prime Minister can converse with the general public. In that sense it is a top down hierarchical communication. But soon after the program ends, the people send in their letters and feedbacks which are later incorporated by the Prime Minister in the next episode of 'Mann ki Baat'.

(b) Participatory Communication

Research has proved that while public can obtain information from impersonal sources like radio and television, this information has relatively little effect on behavioural changes. While the diffusion theory is vertical and top down in its orientation, the participatory model on the other hand stresses the importance of cultural identity of local communities and of *democratization and participation at all levels*—international, national, local and individual (Servaes, 2008).

In order to share information, knowledge, trust, commitment and a right attitude in development projects, participation is very important in any decision-making process for development. Although it is not required that participation means creating and planning the media content, it stresses more on the importance of participation in the decision-making process and selection of the issues to be studied.

"Participation does not imply that there is no longer a role for development specialists, planners, and institutional leaders. It only means that the viewpoint of the local groups of the public is considered before the resources for development projects are allocated and distributed, and that suggestions for changes in the policy are taken into consideration."

-(Servaes, 2008)

Mann ki Baat can be seen as a mix of these above mentioned development communication models. It involves the diffusion of innovations model along with the participatory model.

'Digi Dhan', 'Make in India', Digital India and many more schemes and policies that the government needs the people to implement and acknowledge is spread through this program. Apart from this, awareness about various kinds of diseases and issues are also diffused through 'Mann ki Baat' using radio as the medium.

In this case the program is using radio as a mass medium to influence the masses to use digital technology for transactions and bring about a new practice of innovation within the most rural of areas in the country. In such instances, the Prime Minister, through Radio, encourages people to adopt digital technology and make it a way of life. He talks about digital transactions, schemes, its benefits etc. so that people are made aware of the benefits of this digitisation. Thus, in this sense 'Mann ki Baat' uses a diffusion of innovations model when required, tailored to the specifications of the people and the program.

On the other hand, the program is open to new issues, discussions, problems and ideas that are put forth by the people for whom the program is devised. These people have a say in the decision-making process as they are allowed to voice their achievements, concerns, issues, doubts etc. to the government which is then discussed on the program itself. From using social media to government websites to posting letters, there is nothing that the government has left out when it comes to audience participation. People who are affected by the policies at the grassroot level also have the means to send their feedback and reservations through this program. Also a very important part of effective governance is accountability and communication about what has been done for the people. Also this program creates a feeling of equality and community because there is not an ounce of any kind of discrimination. The PM addresses all his citizens in the same manner and urges all to follow and take to new innovations and practices.

If the mainstream broadcast media also takes up some responsibility and starts holding debates, discussions on those issues and problems that don't cater to a large section of their viewership audience, then this might just help in sensitising the urban audience about the harsh ground realities that exist in the country. Private news channels provide very little segment or time slot for issues of people from backward rural areas or issues of farmers and other rural workers. Environment, cleanliness etc. also do not make the cut for these private channels as they don't work well with TRPs, according to the news channels.

Thus, if these channels start picking up certain issues and hold discussions around it then it will work in the benefit of the society itself. Also once the urban audience is exposed to such news and issues then they will get used to it and the business aspect of these private news channels will not suffer too. It is the cut throat competition and the culture of '24x7 Breaking News' that has led to a sideline of such grave issues.

Conclusion

'Mann ki Baat' is a popular form of development communication. It involves both, diffusion of innovations as well as the participatory model. If the mainstream broadcast media also takes up some responsibility and starts holding debates, discussions on those issues and problems that don't cater to a large section of their viewership audience, then this might just help in sensitising the urban audience about the harsh ground realities that exist in the country.

Also, this show has led to the revival of AIR. Over the years the popularity of Akahsvani saw a dip with the coming of television and then the internet. Their listeners had dropped with response to news and special programes but 'Mann ki Baat' was a fresh new thrust. The revenue of AIR has also increased after it started broadcasting this show.

Apart from that programs like 'Mann ki Baat' should be made more popular so that many more such programs start mushrooming and thus end up increasing awareness, participation, knowledge and use of all sorts of technologies.

REFERENCES

Kaul, V. (2011). DEVELOPMENT COMMUNICATION IN INDIA: PROSPECT, ISSUES AND TRENDS. *Global Media Journal – Indian Edition/ISSN 2249-5835*. Vol.2, 15-24.

Mefalopulos, P. (2008). DEVELOPMENT COMMUNICATION SOURCEBOOK Broadening the Boundaries of Communication. *The World Bank*. 22-45.

Servaes, J. (2008). *Approaches to Development*. SAGE Publications. France.

Ahuja, R. (2016). *Modi's Mann kiBaat is a masterstroke*. Retrieved from - http://www.dailypioneer.com/columnists/oped/modis-mann-ki-baat-is-a-masterstroke.html

Meghalaya Times, (2017). *Modi has managed to revive Radio through Mann kiBaat*. Retrieved at- http://meghalayatimes.info/index.php/editorial/31558-modi-has-managed-to-revive-radio-through-mann-ki-baat

Melkote, S.R. (2006). Theories of Development Communication. In B. Mody(Ed.), *International and Development Communication: A 21st Century Perspective*. Thousand Oaks: Sage Publications.

Kumar, R. (2011). Development Communication: A purposive communication with Social Conscience- an Indian Perspective. *Global Media Journal – Indian Edition*. Winter Issue Vol. 2/No.2

Chakraborty, T. (March 17, 2015). Mann Ki Baat– an Extraordinary Outreach and Bridge: a perspective from a listener. Retrieved from- http://www.spmrf.org/mann-ki-baat-an-extraordinary-outreach-and-bridge-a-perspective-from-a-listener.

Glossary

A-Rate, AA-RATE, and AAA-Rate – levels or classifications of prices charged for advertising in specific time periods or Dayparts. AAA (or Triple-A) is the highest rate, usually charged in peak audience periods or Prime Times. AA (or Double-A) is the next in decreasing order, followed by Single-A Rates. Most Radio Stations that use this type of pricing also include a B Rate, which is the lowest, or least expensive rate assigned to overnight or least demanded time periods.

Acoustics – the properties or qualities of a room or building that determine how sound is transmitted in it. It also refers to the branch of physics concerned with the properties of sound.

Actives – Radio listeners who actively contact radio stations for requests or contests. Passive listeners, however, are those people who do not generally interact with the radio stations.

Ad-ID – is a unique identifier for an advertising spot or other ad entity, which is intended to be the universal industry identifier for all forms of advertising.

Ad-libbing – Words, music, or actions uttered, performed, or carried out extemporaneously in one's own words, without a given script.

Advertising Agency – is business entity that prepares advertising campaigns, plans advertising schedules and places orders with various advertising media.

Air Break – An on-air presentation by a disc jockey.

Aircheck – means demonstration recording by an announcer to showcase their talent. It is also used to refer to off-the-air recordings of broadcasts and also refers to a copy of a broadcast that is recorded on magnetic tape or digitally and also known as audition tapes.

Air Date - the first broadcast of a commercial; also refers to the exact date of a particular TV or radio program.

Air Personality - A disc jockey that works on the air at a radio station

Air shift - is the length of time that a DJ works on the air at any given time. Average air shifts are four hours but could be up to six hours long.

Airtime - amount of time given to a program in radio and television broadcasting.

Airwaves - The medium through which radio or television signals are transmitted. Airwaves are also known by the terms spectrum or the electromagnetic spectrum. Airwave signals travel through the air, unlike the signals transmitted by telephone or cable wires.

AM - Amplitude Modulation, one of two forms of transmitting audio signals to receivers. (The other is FM - Frequency Modulation). This broadcast signal varies the amplitude of the carrier wave. These Stations are frequently referred to as "AM" Stations. An AM Radio Stations assigned to the AM band use Amplitude Modulated Transmitters and Receivers.

Amplification - technological enhancement of sound transmission to increase volume.

Amplifier - An electronic device used to amplify or make sound louder or softer by increasing the voltage, current, or power of a signal.

Analogue - A type of waveform signal with characteristics that are continuous as opposed to pulsed, containing data or information such as voice, data or image. It is the storage or transmission of information by a variable physical means, such as a shift in voltage sent through the electromagnetic spectrum or the vibrations of against patterns inside the grooves of a vinyl disc, to create physical (analogous) patterns of pictures or sounds.

Analogue signals have unpredictable height, or amplitude, and width, frequency, and can vary infinitely over a given range.

Announcer – An on-air talent with the job to read scripts or announcements on radio.

Arbitron (ARB) – A company providing an industry accepted standard for audience measurement of radio programming. Arbitron also refers to the company's Arbitron radio market survey and report that is published four times per year.

Audience – is any group of people exposed to media and in radio broadcasting radio listeners constitute the audience.

Audience Measurement– is a research technique that identifies what kinds of audiences receive a particular kind of media product and how they react to it. The audience is determined according to some variable or set of variables (age, class, gender, ethnicity).

Audio – is a term related to sound or its reproduction; recorded sound material of any kind, including the sound component of a video or film recording.

Audio Branding – means building a brand identity through auditory association techniques, such as jingles and songs.

Audio Consoles – Mixing consoles or a digital mixing console or audio mixer, also called a sound board or soundboard, is an electronic device for combining or mixing, routing, and changing the level, timbre the dynamics of audio signals. A mixer can mix analogue or digital signals depending on the type of mixer.

Audio Sampling Rate – is number of samples per second that are used to digitize a particular sound and measured in Hz or kHz (one kHz being 1 000 Hz). For example, 44100 samples per second can be expressed as either 44100 Hz, or 44.1 kHz.

Audiophile - individual who has an avid interest in stereo or high-fidelity sound recordings.

Audiotape- narrow magnetic tape used to record sound for subsequent playback

Average quarter – A term used in the industry describing audience measurements according to Arbitron - For example, the average number of persons listening to a particular station for at least five minutes during a 15-minute period of time.

Background Music – music that accompanies action or dialogue in a film or television program, usually added at the postproduction stage.

BBC (British Broadcasting Corporation) – one of the first broadcasting systems, established in 1922 in the United Kingdom. The BBC is non-commercial and is, therefore, funded by an annual license fee paid by television owners.

Blackout – means any interruption or exclusion of a broadcast for technical reasons, on account of a labour dispute, or due to government prohibition.

Broadcast – the act of presenting something intended to a wide variety of potential listeners or viewers. This would be the opposite of a "Narrowcast" which is something intended for one or more selected recipients.

Bumper - A song, music, or other element that signals a transition to or from commercial breaks. Bumper music is an example.

Cellular Radio means that radio that receives frequencies that operate in cells according to position. This reception allows car radios to be swapped to the right frequency as the car travels from cell area to cell area.

Combo- two radio stations, usually operated by the same owner in the same market. A Single station is frequently referred to as a "standalone". Three or more commonly owned stations are commonly referred to as a "cluster."

Commentary - news or other report, broadcast live from an event.

Commercial – Advertisement, announcement, spot or message aired on radio which is paid for by an advertiser.

Commercial Break – slot during a radio, television, or Web program during which commercials are broadcast.

CPM (Cost per Million) – Estimate of how much it costs an advertiser to reach a million listeners.

Commercial Radio – Radio run by a privately owned business. In contrast to public and non-profit radio, commercial radio stations sell broadcasting time to advertisers who want to reach listeners. Sponsors pay the stations for time during and between the programs to advertise their products.

Crossfade – A smooth transition between elements.

Cue – Prompting someone to speak. May be verbal or non-verbal

Daypart – the time segments into which a day is divided by radio and television networks and stations for the purpose of selling advertising time. In Radio, the main Dayparts are morning (or AM drive), midday, afternoon (or PM drive) and evening. Advertising contracts should include the specific hours that define the time period for each station's daypart. An individual station's daypart(s) will not necessarily conform to standard definition(s). Stations may also create their own nonstandard or "special" Dayparts.

Standard Radio Dayparts

Morning Drive	-	06:00-AM to 10:00-AM
Mid-day	-	10:00-AM to 03:00-PM
Afternoon Drive	-	03:00-PM to 07:00-PM
Evening	-	07:00-PM to 12:00-AM
Overnight	-	12:00-AM to 06:00-AM

Dead air - On-air silence when there is an error made by the staff or due to equipment failure. It is avoided as listeners may think the station has gone off-air.

Dead Spot- geographic area where radio or television reception is poor, even though it falls within the usual range of the transmitter.

Decibel - a unit used to measure the intensity of a sound.

Digital - means any medium that operates by means of a digital system and also refers to any form of transmission in which a signal is sent in small, separate packages (in contrast to analogue).

Digital Audio Broadcasting (DAB)- is audio broadcasting using digital recordings, which give clearer sound than analogue recordings.

Digital Audio Radio Service (DARS)- is delivery of digital audio signals by satellite directly to homes or automobiles.

Digital Recording- means audio recording made with digital equipment, producing a high-quality clear sound.

DJ or Disk Jockey – is a radio announcer who plays music on air and also refers to anyone who plays recorded music for a specific function.

Docudrama - is dramatization of real-life events (such as the sinking of the Titanic) through film, radio, or television.

Dolby - trademarked electronic circuit that improves the quality of recorded sound by reducing noise.

Drive time - The rush hour commuter periods when radio stations usually have their largest audience. Ad rates are highest for drive time.

Drive-Time Audiences- refers to radio audiences who listen to the radio in their cars in the morning on their way to work or school (usually 6 a.m.–9 a.m.) and in the late afternoon on their way home (usually 4 p.m.–7 p.m.).

Drop-in- A short radio announcement between two songs or two broadcast elements.

Drop-in Ad – is a local commercial inserted into a national program, or, more generally, an advertising message inserted into a larger advertisement, as for a local dealer or retailer, or a phrase, such as a public service slogan, or symbol; also called a hitch-hike ad.

DTH (direct-to-home) - is multichannel broadcast service for television and radio transmitted via communication satellite that subscribers receive directly on their own receivers.

Echo - In audio signal processing and acoustics, echo is a reflection of sound that arrives at the listener with a delay after the direct sound. The delay is proportional to the distance of the reflecting surface from the source and the listener.

Editorial Policy - the stance or position taken by a media outlet on a specific issue or set of issues.

Exclusive Cume–is the number of persons who tune only to one station during a day part.

Fade - To lose audio gradually.

Feed – means to transmit a telecast from one station to other stations or networks.

FM - Frequency Modulation- It is a radio wave broadcast technology that conveys sound – voice and music –using a carrier wave which varies its frequency during transmission, producing high quality audio clarity and tone. Radio Stations assigned to the FM band use Frequency Modulated Transmitters and Receivers. These Stations are frequently referred to as "FM" Stations. The FM frequency range is 88 to 108 MHz.

Folk Music – refers to music style consisting of a people's traditional songs and melodies.

Frequency - The frequency assigned upon which the Radio Station broadcasts. Examples of AM frequency would by 610 kHz. (Kilohertz), while a FM Station might be assigned a frequency of 106.3 MHz (Megahertz).

It also refers to the average number of times the same person will hear a commercial or program within a measured period of time.

Frontsell/Backsell – Frontsell-talk about what's coming up. Backsell-talk about what was just broadcast.

Gag Order – restriction of the publication, discussion, or broadcasting of specific information.

Gain – A term for volume i.e. volume gain.

Grammy Awards – honors given annually for outstanding achievement in music. The first Grammies (the name is an abbreviation of gramophone) were given in 1958. They are now awarded in dozens of categories, from best composition to the best musical arrangement.

Gramophone Machine - used formerly for playing records, invented in 1887 by Emile Berliner, a German immigrant to the United States

Graphic Equalizer- device on an electronic playback machine that allows separate adjustments to be made to the sound quality.

Headphones - pair of earphones joined across the top of a listener's head.

Headset - headphones that have a small microphone for two-way communication, used by television producers, camera persons, and others during filming, taping, or broadcasting.

High Definition Radio (HD Radio) - When two or more stations carry the identical programming, it's called "Simulcasting", but advances in technology now have made it possible for one radio to actually broadcast multiple signals at the same time. This HD Radio concept requires a HD receiver. A listener might be able to listen to one station, and then select one of several formats by going to HD-1, HD-2, HD-3, etc.

Hi-Fi (high fidelity) - reproduction of sound by a radio, CD player, or other device with as little distortion of the original sound as possible.

Hit the Post - is an expression deejays use to describe talking up to the point when the lyrics begin without "stepping" on the beginning of the vocals.

Hook – This is the part of a song that is unique in the listener's ear, such as the portion of the song the listener usually likes and remembers the most.

Hot - In radio terms, something is very loud.

Infomercial - An audio segment that combines advertising with information, sold as a commercial and available on some cable networks and other broadcast media.

Internet Radio- online radio station that either simulcasts versions of on air radio broadcasts over the World Wide Web, or else creates its own programming.

Internet Telephony- system that allows users to make phone calls using the Internet.

Interview - encounter during which a journalist or a radio or television announcer asks someone relevant questions about a topic.

Intonation - melodic patterns built into utterances for specific effects or communicative purposes (to express surprise, doubtfulness, etc.).

Intro - In radio terms, the start of a broadcast element.

Jingle - A programming element such as an anthem or musical song produced by professional studio singers for commercials or radio station promotional announcements.

Karaoke - form of entertainment in which people sing popular songs accompanied by pre-recorded music, played by a machine that may also display the words on a screen.

Level – The volume level that controls the broadcast.

Libel - refers to false and malicious statement that damages a person's reputation; and published or broadcast statement that unjustifiably exposes someone to ridicule or derision.

Liner – A written phrase that stand by themselves and are meant to communicate concise imaging. Typically, a DJ says a "liner" over an intro of a record or during a commercial break between songs and spots.

Live - broadcasting of an event as it unfolds.

Live Assist – This describes how a DJ creates a radio show by interacting with a computerized system. The DJ provides live talk, chat, liners, and then activates the computer system which automatically runs commercial spots, jingles, promos or songs. When it is time for the DJ to talk again, he/she deactivates the automation and goes live again.

Log – The written record of what transpires at the radio station, including: music, commercial content and transmitting specifications. A music log is a list of the songs played for the day, a commercial log shows which commercials were played and when and an engineering log show the status of a transmitter's specifications during the course of a day.

Low Power FM (LPFM) - A broadcast service that permits the licensing of 50-100 watt FM radio stations within a service radius of up to 3.5 miles and 1-10 watt FM radio stations within a service radius of 1 to 2 miles, commonly used in community radio broadcasting.

Marconi, Guglielmo (1874-1937) - Italian inventor who popularized wireless telegraphy, known shortly thereafter as radio.

Microphone (mic) - is a device that changes sound into electrical current, which instantly travels over wires or through the air to a loudspeaker or some other device that changes it back into sound. The first microphone was the telephone transmitter, invented by Alexander Graham Bell in 1876. Today, microphones are used in public-address systems and in radio and television broadcasting. They are also used in recording the sound for motion pictures, in making compact discs, and in webcasting.

Microphone Polar Patterns - Polar patterns describe how microphones pick up sound, showing specifically where mics 'listen' spatially and which positions are blocked. Having a good grasp of these polar patterns will help you select the right mics that capture the sound that you need while minimizing unwanted noise.

Cardioid Microphones - capture everything in front and block everything else. This front-focused pattern will let the operator to point the mic to a sound source and isolate it from unwanted ambient sound, making it ideal for live performance and other situations where noise reduction and feedback suppression are needed.

Super/Hyper Cardioid Microphones - have the same front directionality, but have a narrower area of sensitivity compared to cardioids. This results in improved isolation and higher resistance to feedback. Because of their enhanced ability to reject noise, it can be used for loud sound sources, noisy stage environments or even for untreated recording rooms.

Omnidirectional Microphones - are microphones that capture sound from all angles. Because of their non-directional design and zero rejection, these mics capture nuances better, resulting in a more natural sound. These mics can be used in studios and other venues with great acoustics, and for live recording of multiple instruments, as long as the noise level is low.

Figure-8 Microphones - The name of this pattern is derived from its graphical representation, which looks like the number 8. Figure-8 mics capture the sound of both the front and back, while rejecting the two sides.

Shotgun mics, also called Line and Gradient, feature a tube like design that make their polar pattern even more directional than hyper cardioids. This design results in a tighter polar pattern up front with longer pickup range.

Switchable/Multi-Pattern Microphones are microphones that can change between different polar patterns, allowing for versatile placement. Many of today's USB condenser microphones have this feature, letting the operator to switch between multiple patterns by simply flicking a switch.

Condenser mics have a thin conductive diaphragm that sits close to a metal backplate. This configuration works like a capacitor wherein sound pressure vibrates the diaphragm which in turn changes the capacitance to produce the audio signal. Since they use capacitance instead of actual moving coils, fidelity and sound quality is improved, making these mics ideal for precision recording in the studio. This method of sound capture requires power, so it needs a mixer or direct box with phantom power.

Megabyte - unit of computer memory equal to one million bytes.

Metal Music - type of rock music characterized by highly amplified electric guitars, a hard beat, a thumping bass, and often dark lyrics.

Mixing - putting together different excerpts of audio, such as vocal commentary and music, to create a final piece for broadcasting.

Modulation - system designed to increase the frequency of signals. The two main types of modulation are called amplitude modulation (AM) and frequency modulation (FM).

Multicasting - This is the ability of one Radio Station to actually broadcast several different program channel simultaneously using HD Radio. It is the exact opposite of Simulcasting. Rather than several stations carrying the identical programming, multicasting allows One Station to carry multiple streams of programming from the same Transmitter.

Multitrack - device or system capable of using different tracks in sound recording or reproduction.

Musical - theatrical production that revolves around the music composed for it.

Narrator – The individual who announces/narrates during the course of a broadcast program.

Narrowcasting - broadcasting directed at a limited target audience.

Obscene Language – it is a term that is most often used in a legal context to describe expressions (words, images, actions) that offend the prevalent sexual morality of the time. It can simply be used to mean profanity, or it can mean anything taboo, indecent, abhorrent, or disgusting. (Latin: obscenus, meaning "foul, repulsive, detestable.")

Offthe Record - comments made spontaneously and not intended to be published or broadcast.

Off-Air - events or dialogue taking place in a broadcasting studio but not put on the air.

On Demand Audio – is the act of streaming or turning audio into digital data and transmitting it over the Internet.

On the Beach – it is a radio industry term for being unemployed.

Online Radio- Radio programming transmitted over the Internet instead of the airwaves. Most online radio is either traditional radio stations simulcasting their signal or original stations broadcasting exclusively on the Web. Unlike traditional radio, online radio does not require a special receiver to access the content. Any computer with Internet access can be used tolisten to online radio.

Open Mic – A microphone which is live, on at the given moment.

Outro - In radio terms, the finish of something.

Payola - Illegal practice of taking payment or other benefits to play certain songs on the radio and not identifying the sponsorship. Payola scandals have been common in the radio broadcast industry from the 1950s to the early 2000s. As playlists are now rarely chosen by the DJs themselves and are delivered pre-recorded by companies, there is less opportunity for payola.

PD (Program Director) - is the individual who controls the radio station's format or programs that are broadcast.

Playlist –is the list of songs that a station will play. It is often programmed by a company and even pre-recorded to run in order, with slots for commercial breaks and talk.

PSA (Public Service Announcement) - is an ad that is run in the public interest rather than for a commercial product of service.

Phone In - is radio program that receives phone calls from audience members, who are encouraged to ask the host or guest questions, make comments, or take part in a discussion.

Phone Interface – is an electronic device allowing on-air performers easy access to telephone lines. It allows the audio signal from a microphone to be heard by a caller and takes the caller's audio and directs it into a radio studio console or recording device.

Pitch – The actual tone or sound of one's voice.

PJ – A slang term that means a Pod-Jockey or a PJ for a Podcaster one who hosts a podcast containing music.

Player – A software application that can receive audio streams over the Internet and convert the digital data back into sound. For example music, talk, etc.

Play-by-Play Announcing – The main sports announcer on a sports event broadcast, responsible for describing the plays as they happen. Usually works with a colour announcer who supplies descriptions, anecdotes and background information during pauses in play.

Podcast - An audio file in a concise form like an .mp3, created in the form of a radio program with a way to subscribe to it, so it is downloaded from the Internet and delivered to a personal audio device, such as an iPod/Computer for playback.

Pop Music- Popular music means music intended to be appreciated by ordinary people, usually intended to provide entertainment and pleasure, and including such genres as jazz, swing, rhythm and blues, rock, and rap. Pop music surfaced at the start of the twentieth century, spreading in the 1920s with the rise of jazz music.

Pre-Production- work to be done before the recording stage of a text or program, such as scripting and budgeting.

Primary Coverage - is the area where the reception of a broadcast is at its best; an excellent locality and area.

Producer - The person at a radio station who conducts the day-to-day business for a radio show, from lining up guests to acting as a liaison between management and talent.

Production - work of putting together a media text in a format. (Video, Radio, Film etc...)

Production Element - means an audio element such as music, a sound effect, or an audio effect, including a reverb or echo, used in creating a final audio mix such as a commercial, promotional announcement, or even a humorous skit.

Production Director - The person at a radio station responsible for overseeing the creation and implementation of commercial content, promotional announcements and any other audio element that must be created for broadcast.

Production Manager - The person who is in charge of producing the commercial announcements.

Programming - The output or product of a radio station that is presented either in long form or short form styles. An example of long form programming is when a station presents a topic in extended length, such as public radio does. Short form programming is when a station maintains a constant format, such as a style of music where the programming includes smaller modules strung together.

Promo – An announcement, live or pre-recorded, promoting upcoming events or the radio station's image, promotes the results of a past event or promotes any other event which benefits a station's activities.

Promotions Director – is the individual who is responsible for creating, planning and carrying out the logistics of both sales and programming oriented promotions.

Propaganda - materials, strategies, etc. (overt or covert), used to spread particular ideologies or opinions in order to convince or persuade people of their validity.

Public Interest – Refers to a concept suggesting that in return for using the public airwaves free of charge, a broadcaster is obligated to act as a trustee of public property and do what is best for the public good. The "public" refers to the local community to which broadcasters are licensed to serve, while "interest" means to benefit the public, as distinct from programs the public is interested in. Public interest obligations are those specific actions broadcasters undertake in exchange for their free license to repay the public for using the broadcast spectrum of public airwaves.

Queue – a number of cuts or commercials that are waiting to be played back in a specific, predetermined manner as in a station break.

Quiz Show - radio or television show designed to test the knowledge, luck, or skill of contestants or experts.

Quadraphonic - four-channel (four speaker) sound system.

Radio–refers to transmission of sounds converted into electromagnetic waves directly through space to a receiving device, which converts them back into sounds.

Radio Format – is the type of music and programming broadcast by a radio station. These can include news, talk, sports, country, contemporary, rock, alternative, urban, classical, religious, or college.

Radio Frequency - radio frequency spectrum is the portion of the electromagnetic spectrum that is used for all radio, wireless communication, and television channels.

Radio Station - is a place from which a radio broadcast originates. There are two main types of radio stations: commercial and public. The former are owned by private companies, making profits from advertisements; the latter are funded by the government. Some countries also have non-profit stations called community radio stations, operated mainly by NGOs and educational institutions.

Rap musical style in which lyrics are rapped (chanted) to rhythmic musical accompaniment, associated in its origin with African American youth.

Recording - permanent copy of music on a disc, CD, DVD, or other device.

Reportage - refers to use of a medium (print, broadcast, Internet) to present the news; corpus of news; and a style of reporting news.

Reverberation - in psychoacoustics and acoustics, is the persistence of sound after a sound is produced. A reverberation, or reverb, is created when a sound or signal is reflected causing a large number of reflections to build up and then decay as the sound is absorbed by the surfaces of objects in the space - which could include furniture, people, and air.

Satellite Radio - radio stations, such as Sirius and XM that broadcast via satellite and usually operate on a pay-per-service basis.

Script - written text of a play, screenplay, or broadcast, used in production or performance.

Script Doctor - writer who is asked to improve a script written by someone else, to make it conform to production expectations.

Short-Wave Radio - radio that transmits waves that have lengths shorter than those of waves used in amplitude modulation (AM) transmissions. Short waves carry frequency modulation (FM) radio broadcasts and television signals.

Signature Tune – or theme song is a musical theme used to introduce a radio show.

Slander - any untrue or misleading statement that damages someone's reputation.

Slang - refers to any language used by certain groups (such as adolescents) for purposes of group identity; and informal speech in general. In the twentieth century, the mass media have been instrumental in spreading slang broadly.

Sound Bite – A brief statement or excerpt from an interview for use in radio news program.

Sound - vibrations that travel through the air or another medium and can be heard when they reach a person's or animal's ear.

Sound Card- expansion card that can convert analogue sound (as from a microphone or audio tape) to digital form, or convert digitized audio signals (as from an audio file) to analogue signals that can be played on a computer's speakers.

Sound Effects– means imitations of natural and other kinds of sounds to accompany the action and to suggest realism in a movie, play, or program.

Sound Image – is any sound that is perceived or interpreted in the same way as a picture.

Soundtrack - refers to narrow band recorded on the side of the film image; and general term for the dialogue, music and sound effects in a film or video.

Speech - the use of language in face to face conversations, in writing, etc.

Spot - A radio commercial. Spot announcements refer to commercial or public service announcements that are placed on television or radio programs.

Stereo - (stereophonic sound) any electronic audio playback system that is capable of reproducing high-quality sound that comes from various directions (usually through speakers).

Stop Set - The slots for commercials during the broadcast hour. They may be recurring and of the same length. They may be filled by paid advertising spots or by public service announcements. Stop Set length can vary much between local stations and even network programming.

Surround Sound - also called *ambisonics* is recording and playback system that uses three or more channels or speakers in order to create the effect of sound surrounding the listener.

Tape- plastic thin layer used for recording and playing back sound.

Target Audience - group at whom a specific media product or advertising strategy is directed.

Telephone - device designed for simultaneous transmission and reception of the human voice. In 1876 the Scottish born American inventor Alexander Graham Bell patented the first telephone.

Tonality - refers to organization of music around a tone.

Tone - in music, sound made by the vibration of a musical instrument or of the human voice.

Transmission - sending messages to a receiver.

Tune - refers to a melody and a catchy popular song.

UHF (Ultra High Frequency)- type of short radio wave widely used in television broadcasting. UHF waves also are used in aircraft and ship navigation, in emergency communications systems, and cellular telephone networks.

Underwriting - is the term used in Public Radio and other non-commercial stations for the on air creditsor acknowledgments for financial support from a business, individual or organization.

Urban Music- pop music genres that appeal to an urban audience, including rhythm and blues and hip-hop. Urban is one of radio's more popular formats.

VHF (Very High Frequency) - electromagnetic waves assigned to television and frequency modulation (FM) radio stations and to amateur radio operators.

Voice - refers to sound made by human vocalcords.

Voice of America (VOA)- is a U.S. government-funded broadcasting system, launched in 1942 that provides radio, television, and Internet services, especially news, in over 40 languages.

Voice-Over-Internet-Protocol (VoIP) refers to technology that allows voice messages to be sent via the Internet.

Voiceover – A production technique using a disembodied voice as broadcast live or pre-recorded in radio programs. Voiceovers can also be commonly referred to as an off camera commentary.

Voice Track – means a pre-recorded voice of a radio personality or DJ that is recorded and stored in a computer to be played at a specific time in a pre-programmed sequence such as at the beginning or end of a song.

Vocal/Voice Exercises – Exercises that help prepare the breath to support the voice.

Voice and Speech Training – is intended for speech and voice improvement for professional and public speaking, foreign accent reduction, and communication etiquette.

Volume – means the loudness of voice/sound. The higher the intensity of a sound, the louder it is perceived in our ears, and the higher volume it has.

VU (Volume Unit) Meter – is a device which measures, in units, the strength of an audio signal.

Walkie-Talkie - two-way radio enabling voice communication over short distances.

Weather Reporting – Broadcasts on radio or television about local daily weather, or for local and national weather service warnings and watches.

Wire Services – News and press release distribution services.

Write In – Added to a script or to a commercial copy in addition to the script.

White Noise - radio noise spread over a wide range of frequencies.

Word Painting- technique used in the radio broadcast industry that uses highly descriptive words during dramatizations to evoke images in reading material as an attempt to place the listener into the scene.

XM Satellite Radio - founded in 1992 as American Mobile Radio Corporation, a satellite service in the United States and Canada providing pay-for service radio programming, with music, news, sports, talk, entertainment, and weather channels. Most of the channels are available via the Internet. XM also offers music downloads.

Acknowledgement: The glossary of radio broadcasting is compiled from *Dictionary of Media and Communications* by Marcel Danesi and websites likewww. radioconnection. com, http://www.tdga.org, http://www.qsl.net, and www.thoughtco.com.

Compilation: **Dr. Albert Abraham**

Index